Sacred
JOURNEYS

Ecumenical Perspectives on Spiritual Care

Michael J. Kurtz, PhD

WESTBOW
PRESS®
A DIVISION OF THOMAS NELSON
& ZONDERVAN

WestBow Press books may be ordered through booksellers or by contacting:

WestBow Press
A Division of Thomas Nelson & Zondervan
1663 Liberty Drive
Bloomington, IN 47403
www.westbowpress.com
1 (866) 928-1240

ISBN: 978-1-9736-1264-3 (sc)
ISBN: 978-1-9736-1265-0 (hc)
ISBN: 978-1-9736-1266-7 (e)

Library of Congress Control Number: 2017919753

Print information available on the last page.

WestBow Press rev. date: 01/04/2018

Contents

Contents

Dedicated to all those called to bring
spiritual care to a broken world.

Acknowledgements

Illustrations were selected and designed by Mary C. McKiel. I appreciate Mary sharing her skill and passion for photography to benefit this project. All illustrations are publicly available and royalty free.

I am grateful for the wonderful support I received from my wife, Cherie. She provided critical assistance in preparing and doing the initial review of the text. Her skill and love are deeply appreciated.

Introduction

The idea for this collection of essays came to me rather suddenly in the summer of 2016. Most likely, this idea of essays written by skilled spiritual care providers had been rumbling below my consciousness for some time. In the midst of so much violence and dissent across the globe, the idea of reflections rooted in the universal values of peace, kindness, service to others, and tolerance felt totally restorative to the spirit.

I thought a variety of perspectives rooted in diverse backgrounds and experiences would be most valuable for readers. From this has come essays by spiritual care practitioners in the Jewish, Christian, and Islamic traditions whose formative experiences in Central Asia, Europe, Africa, and the United States have shaped their ministries in service to the people of God.

The essays in this collection are intensely personal and very different, one from another. Yet the spirit of service, the love and care for God's people, and the hope in God's transformative power radiate through each one. I hope these essays touch the hearts and minds of readers from a wide variety of experiences and life situations. Individuals considering entering spiritual care ministry or who have been engaged for many years will find nurture, inspiration, and hope in these essays. I believe that the values lived and expressed by the authors will prove meaningful to readers whether or not they are religious in a traditional sense.

At the end of the book is a section about the authors that provides biographical backgrounds on the essayists. But, in truth, the real biographical insights are found in each essay. God's hand and the writers' own spirit of service led each of them on long journeys of self-discovery, gaining the wisdom and experience they now seek to share. The life stories differ as do the ministries undertaken. But, in a very real way, the essays are congruent. Each one is filled with a sense of self-awareness, reflection, and wonder at the ways in which God has used the writers to reach people caught in a variety of conflicts and struggles.

The essayists leave us, the readers, with a sense of hope. It is possible with God's help, rigorous training, and the willingness to learn from our struggles and doubts to be a force for healing and good in this world. This is the message that unites the essays. Whether the traditions be Roman Catholic, American Protestant, Reformed Judaism, or Islamic, under the surface of differences we are all one. The ministries shared in these essays take place in parish settings, in hospitals, in schools, on the streets, and in locales near and far.

But the essays share the sublime and critical point that we are all one in the human condition. Our hopes and our fears are the same the world over. What the authors inspire us to do, regardless of our background or calling, is to take a leap of faith in reaching out to others. We are called in these essays to take the risk of listening to the pain and fear of others, to risk the opening of our hearts, and to be ambassadors of God's love to a hurting world.

The authors make clear that this path is not an easy one, but there is a joy and sense of peace that radiates from these shared reflections. May the stories that fill these essays nurture and inspire each and every one of us.

Spiritual Care: An Overview

Michael J. Kurtz, PhD

Spiritual needs are as ancient as humankind. And just as ancient is the impulse, the imperative, to respond to those in distress. The need for healing and the empowerment of love—for others, the self, and for God—is universal. Providing guidance in living lives of care and purpose, in finding the spiritual resources to heal life's wounds, and in coping with adversity is a continuing challenge in every age. Humanity always confronts the deepest existential questions: Why do I exist? Why am I ill? Will I die? What will happen to me when I die?

For millennia, spirituality and religion were considered basically one and the same. This is not true in the modern era. Many reject formal religious dogmas and practices but feel a deep need for connection or a relationship with others, with nature, and with some higher source, whatever that may be. The deepest human needs remain, and so does the call to respond to those needs. The behaviors that reflect the deeper impulses of our spiritual selves include practicing altruism, praying, forgiving, and some form of contemplation or meditation. Our quest for meaning in life, our spirituality, provides us a real inner resilience that helps us cope with life's challenges.[1] Yet whether an individual is actively engaged in organized religion or on his or her own spiritual journey, the great Abrahamic faiths—Judaism, Christianity, and Islam—have profound lessons rooted in deep spiritual understanding for those who suffer and those who seek to bring a healing touch.

In Judaism, the foundational texts for spiritual care are found in the Hebrew Bible: in Genesis 1:1 and 18:1, and in Ezekiel 34:11–12. In Genesis 1, the Lord God created the heavens and the earth, and in 18:1 he shows his care for his nation, Israel. In Ezekiel, God describes himself as a shepherd concerned for all the sheep. In Jewish classical texts—Midrash, Mishnah, and Talmud—rabbis and scholars, such as Rabbi Akiva, Rabbi Dimi, and Nachmanides, developed key concepts on the moral imperatives to aid the sick and the dying.[2]

The key spiritual care concept *bikkur holim*, the sick visit, is more than a friendly visit. It is a healing intervention with prayer and the practical assistance that the sick and the dying require. To visit and aid the sick is to imitate God. In short, bikkur holim is a pragmatic, practical, and spiritual intervention. All this goes with the injunction *gemilut chasadim*, to perform deeds of loving kindness.[3]

In the Jewish tradition, Moses (Isa. 63:11) and David (1 Chron. 11:2) are portrayed as shepherds expressing God's loving care for his people.[4] Similarly, Jesus refers to himself as the Good Shepherd (John 10:14). The fundamental texts for Christians that describe the essential qualities of pastoral or spiritual caregivers are found in the pastoral epistles of St. Paul. The apostle Peter urged leaders in the newly formed Christian communities to "shepherd the flock of God that is among

---

[1] Sarah E. Koss and Mark D. Holder, "Toward a Global Understanding of Spirituality and Religiosity: Definitions, Assessments, and Benefits," in *Global Practices, Societal Attitudes, and Effects in Health*, ed. Edith G. Roberts (New York: Nova Science Publishers, 2015), 214–19.

[2] Rabbi Charles Steer, "Bikkur Holim: The Origins of Jewish Pastoral Care," *Journal of Health Care Chaplaincy* 15 no. 2 (2009): 100–104.

[3] Rabbi Dayle E. Friedman, ed., *Jewish Pastoral Care: A Practical Handbook*, 2nd ed. (Jewish Lights Publishing, 2015), xiv.

[4] Ibid., xvi.

you, exercising oversight, not under compulsion, but willingly, as God would have you; not for shameful gain, but eagerly; not domineering over those in your charge, but being examples to the flock" (1 Peter 5:2–3 ESV).[5]

Christian pastoral care has deep roots in biblical psychology with its understanding of people, problems, and solutions developed from a theological perspective. Perhaps the most evocative expression of pastoral care in America is found in the African American experience, with its theology of suffering. Soul care and spiritual direction enabled those who endured slavery and what came after to experience "shared sorrow as endured sorrow."[6]

Pastoral and spiritual caregivers knew that what the flock needed was not speeches but empathetic listening and understanding. Believers in this particular component of the Christian tradition understood that "God uses unjust to make us just, unloving treatment to make us more loving, and arrogant abusers to make us more humble."[7]

The concept of pastoral and spiritual care is central to the third Abrahamic faith tradition—Islam. Each of the Abrahamic traditions has its way of defining their unique method of caregiving and of extending oneself to aid in alleviating the suffering of others. In Islam, the teachings of the Prophet Muhammad are foundational. In the Qur'an (9:71), the followers of the faith are commanded to cooperate toward goodness. In the Bukhari, a book of the traditions of the Prophet, believers are told that "none of you have Faith till he loves for his brother what he loves for himself."[8]

Various stories in literature make it clear that the Prophet teaches that visiting the sick should be offered to all, friend or foe. Though there are many interpretations of Islam, as there are in Judaism and Christianity, all are required to visit and support the ill and distressed.

---

[5] English Standard Version Study Bible.

[6] Robert Kellemen and Karole A. Edwards, *Beyond the Suffering: Embracing the Legacy of African-American Soul Care and Spiritual Direction* (Baker Books, 2007), 31.

[7] Ibid., 55–56.

[8] Chaplain Asgar Rajput, "Pastoral Care in Higher Education: Muslim Involvement in the History of Chaplaincy," *Academia*, 24.

Visits are to be short, with words carefully chosen to offer support and hope. Prayer is an essential ingredient to every visit.[9]

All the great Abrahamic faiths command followers to give alms or aid to the poor, feed the needy, honor the dead by attending funerals, and be kind to neighbors. Each tradition exhorts its followers, in the Hebrew term *livui ruchani*, to "walk with another."[10] This is sharing the burden with those who are experiencing suffering and illness. This love of neighbor is a command for all believers, not just those who are part of the religious establishment.

In contemporary America, the Jewish, Christian, and Islamic faiths are engaged in the "love of neighbor" through synagogues, churches, mosques, and countless community organizations. Spiritual care is intrinsic to all these endeavors. There is one avenue of spiritual care, clinical pastoral education (CPE), that increasingly engages caregivers from all three traditions. CPE began as an American Protestant movement in the first half of the twentieth century, and it was designed to integrate theological and pastoral traditions with insight from contemporary psychology. CPE services are provided in hospitals, prisons, and private counseling, among many other venues.

One of the founders of CPE, Anton Boisen, wrote about the "human living document"— that is, seeing the whole person—mind, body, and spirit—as a living text requiring careful and sensitive understanding to develop an effective pastoral response.[11] This, in many ways, is congruent with the spirit of the textual documents that are foundational for the three Abrahamic traditions. Over time, the CPE movement has expanded to the various denominations of Christianity as well as to the Jewish and Muslim faiths. Among the national associations of CPE providers and chaplains, there is now the National Association of Jewish Chaplains and the Association of Muslim Chaplains.[12]

---

[9] Ibid.

[10] Friedman, *Jewish Pastoral Care*, xvii.

[11] E. Brooks Holifield, *A History of Pastoral Care in America: From Salvation to Self-Realization* (Nashville: Abingdon Press, 1983), 244–47.

[12] Adapted from materials in the *Encyclopedia Judaica* (2008) and "Muslim Chaplaincy in the U.S.," http://pluralism.org.

The concept of spiritual care is inherent in all three faiths. The need to listen to those who are suffering from whatever ailments afflict them and to respond with care, offering hope and spiritual consolation, is at the heart of religious traditions that are millennia old. All believers, not just clergy, are called to "love your neighbor" in practical and concrete ways. Caregiving is never easy. It challenges us to provide comfort, "coming alongside to lend support and to instill courage in a hurting heart."[13]

We all, each one of us, have the potential and the responsibility to be spiritual caregivers. We may or may not be members of the clergy or affiliated with an organized religious group. Whatever our circumstances, we encounter fellow travelers suffering grief, loss, illness, economic deprivation, persecution, or spiritual desolation. For me, the example of other caregivers provides me with the role models of compassion who aid in turning aspiration into service—role models who teach by example the moral imperative to love, the discipline to listen, and the heart to respond.

The essayists in this volume come from varied backgrounds and traditions. The stories they share are different from one another, but the love and hope they share are a light in an often-dark world. We will all benefit from their wisdom, experience, and compassion.

---

[13] Kelleman and Edwards, *Beyond the Suffering*, Grand Rapids, Michigan, 32.

God's Icy Clay

Rev. John G. Lynch, PhD

So I went down to the house of a potter,
and found him working at the wheel,
and if the vessel he was making was spoiled,
as happens to clay in the potter's hands,
he would make it into another vessel,
such as the potter saw fit to make.
—Jeremiah 18:3–4 (Jewish Publication Society Translation)

When I crawled out from my Roman Catholic seminary training at age twenty-seven, I really believed God had shaped me into a fine vessel for his Word. God, however, took one look at me and said, "John, your clay is way too icy and brittle—too much church law and textbook ethics. I'm going to put you back on my wheel, melt your clay down, and reshape you into a gospel man. Guess where I'm going to do this? Paris! So jump on that plane and get moving."

My New York to Paris flight hit the tarmac dancing. Everyone in Paris danced that night. Nineteen years earlier, on August 25, 1944, the Germans had surrendered. The next day, Charles de Gaulle, General Leclerc, and a host of French officers had led the French army on a victory march down the Champs-Élysées. The day I arrived, Notre Dame cathedral smiled down on a thousand dancers in the streets.

6

Soon after, God sent me to Montmartre. As I stepped from the metro station called Abbesses, new rhythms pulsed through the air. Five blocks away stood the gaudy Moulin Rouge. Its cabaret drumbeats flowed over into our Abbesses neighborhood, where fifty thousand people lived crammed into small apartments in six-floor walk-ups, a part of Paris that most American tourists never see. I was about to begin two years as a parish vicar at the Christian Community of St. John of Montmartre. Our church sat just across from a small park populated mostly with teenage gang members and lots of wise older women. They were the people God sent to melt and reshape my clay.

They taught me what I desperately needed to know as a pastor and a priest: (1) be a listener, (2) watch one hour with people in their gardens of Gethsemane, (3) street ethics trump textbook ethics every time, and (4) "For freedom, Christ has set us free." (Galatians 5:1 ESV).

Be a Listener

Our church built a small, storefront office. A sign read "*Pretre de garde,*" a take-off on the phrase *chien de garde* (watchdog). The Holy Spirit moved me to serve as the watchdog priest every chance I had. People from the square came in to talk. I listened. The teenagers in the street gangs wanted to speak to me about the Americans they loved best—Al Capone, John Dillinger, and Baby Face Nelson, no matter that I barely understood a word they said. Listening to unknown words forced me into a deeper level of hearing. I learned to connect with the feelings behind the words, where heart speaks to heart. I caught their enthusiasm about American gangsters. They really appreciated my sympathetic ear. I felt what they said, and that was enough.

One day a woman came in to tell me, for forty-five minutes, how upset she was about the islands of Jersey and Guernsey. *What?* I thought. *Why is she coming in to speak to me, a priest, about Jersey and Guernsey? Speak to me about Jesus or God or ethics, but not two small islands in the English Channel!* Fortunately, I said nothing. I just listened.

She finished by saying, "Those horrible English stole them from us a long time ago. They're still French! It's not right. It breaks my heart to see those small parts of France still in English hands." As she rose to leave, I started to understand just a little bit how she felt about the situation. "Thank you so much for listening," she said. I had not said a word. Many years later when I served a small church in Pasadena, Maryland, another woman said the same thing. "Thank you for listening, pastor," she said. "I always feel better when I run my mouth."

Many times, since those early days in Montmartre, I have listened to anguished, stressed-out people without saying a word. I start to feel as they feel, and that makes all the difference.

"Watch One Hour with Me"

We had ten priests on the staff at St. John of Montmartre—seven French, one Italian, one Basque, and one American. We "foreigners," all students at the Catholic University of Paris, had our home at the parish and worked there part-time to help out. Most of the French priests focused their ministry on like-minded groups of people—young adults, married couples, or liturgy people. They never wore cassocks on the streets, as priests had always done for centuries.

But one of the Frenchmen, Francois Lorentz, an Alsatian, always wore his cassock on the street. The first person to speak English with me when I arrived, he liked to read Charles Dickens in English. He never worked with groups. All his ministry was one on one. He served as the "patronage" priest, in which role he supervised an after-school program for forty to fifty kids. He knew them all by name, and he knew all their families. On Thursdays, when schools were closed, he often took them all on commuter trains out to the country. For many of these kids, Pere Lorentz was their only gate out of the city.

One Saturday our whole team gathered for the main meal (always at 1:00 p.m.). As we were talking about the groups with whom most of the French priests worked, suddenly fire trucks and ambulances raced down the Rue des Abbesses just under our dining room window. Francois Lorentz jumped from the table and hurried out, his black robe fluttering in the breeze. Nobody else moved. God pushed me out the door to follow him. We ran three blocks and then up two flights to a small apartment. Firemen were trying to resuscitate a ten-year-old boy who had drowned in his kitchen bathtub.

"I know him," Francois said. "This is Martin. I have been instructing him for baptism. Should I baptize him?"

The firemen said, "I think he's gone, Monsieur l'Abbe."

"I would," I said.

He baptized Martin. Three older women came into the room. "Help us put him in this bed," they said to me. As I reached under his arms to lift him, I heard water gurgle down his throat. "Now please close his eyes," they continued. With shaking hands, I brushed his eyelids down to close his eyes. He had big, blue eyes. The firemen left. After a while, Francois left. God, however, riveted me to the floor, and I just couldn't move.

About an hour later, the boy's grandmother came up for her weekly visit with her grandson. She saw me and started to scream. "What has happened? Why is the priest here?" She fell into my arms, and she cried and cried and cried. Four hours later, Father Bruno from the church came in and said, "John, why don't you go home now? You need some rest."

For four hours, I had sat by Martin's grandmother, mother, and aunt as they lived their gardens of Gethsemane. I didn't say a word. I just watched with them.

Many years later, while serving as a seminary professor at St. Paul's College in Washington, DC, I noticed a huge difference between my students who had gone through CPE and those who had not. The CPE guys had heart. I wanted to find out what this CPE was all about, so I served one summer as a chaplain in a mental hospital near Atlanta. Almost every day I visited a patient who sat all day staring at a spot on the carpet. He never spoke, nor did I. After a while, we both sat there staring for twenty or thirty minutes at the same spot! The day before I was to leave, I sat next to him, expecting another half hour of shared silence. He turned his head and said, "Thank you so much for our visits. They've meant a lot to me." Sometimes the best thing we can do as pastors is shut up and watch one hour with people in their gardens of Gethsemane.

"Street Ethics Trumps Book Ethics Every Time"

Gerard came one Friday in November. "Father," he said, "I'm not asking you for absolution in confession. I know you can't give it to me. My partner and I have been together for fifteen years. My wife and daughter live in another city. They know about us, and they know we're not breaking up. I'm coming for Communion on Sunday in your communion line. I know you're not supposed to give me communion unless we break up our homosexual relationship. I'm not doing that. But I'm sick of just going to Mass without receiving communion. So I will be in your communion line on Sunday, and I hope you'll give me communion. If you don't, I'll understand." He knew what my seminary ethics textbooks said, and so did I. My heart told me, *Give him communion!"* My head, still buried in those bookish ethics, said, *No way—you know the rules, and so does he.*

When Sunday came, I saw him coming down the aisle with tears in his eyes. I could not let him pass. "The body of Christ," I said, placing the host on his tongue. "Amen," he whispered. That whispered *amen* rang through the heavens like a thunderclap. *Thank God!* cried the angels. *Another priest has followed his heart and kicked his textbook ethics into the trash can of hell, where it belongs.* I never saw Gerard again.

"For Freedom, Christ Has Set Us Free" (Gal. 5:1 ESV)

Our teen boys' youth group buzzed across the English Channel and then boarded an overnight train to Scotland. There, at the foot of Ben Nevis, the highest mountain in the British Isles, we camped in a field for a week. That night in Fort William, when the boys from Paris met the girls from Scotland, their teenage hormones blazed like the Northern lights across the Highlands. The next morning, I walked along a narrow road with Marcel. "I know what I did last night was a sin," he said, "but it was beautiful, and I did it beautifully."

"Marcel," I protested, "it was either beautiful or a sin. It can't be both."

"Then," he replied, "it was beautiful. *C'est tout.* (That's all there is to it!)"

My seminary textbooks, church, and family had insisted that sex between teenagers is risky, irresponsible, and sinful. Through sixteen-year-old Marcel, God told me, *Your textbooks, church, and family need revising; so do your glacier-like views on sexuality. When it comes to sexual ethics, I speak more through personal experiences than through a thousand textbooks, churches, or inherited family values.* When I shared this story with my wife many decades later, she said, "Well, Marcel certainly spoke to you, but I'd like to know how the Scottish girl felt about their experience. She might be more interested in the long-term view." She's right, of course; there's more to sexuality than "It's beautiful." But up there in Scotland, I needed to hear what Marcel said. He started the meltdown on my ice-bound views on sex. I have never forgotten him or that moment of grace.

"No Longer Do I Call You Servants ... But I Have Called You Friends" (John 15:15 ESV)

After I left Montmartre, the Lord still had one important edge of my stiff clay to knock down and rebuild. It all began when I met a priest friend mine who told me, "I've gotten married since I saw you last."

"Married!" I cried out "How can you be married? You're a priest, and priests can't be married!"

"Well, I am," he said. "I serve as a priest here, and I live in another city with my wife."

The next day I met with him and his wife. "This is a scandal," I protested. "Someone will find out, and your whole congregation will be scandalized."

"We told you this in confidence," he answered, "so don't be blowing any whistles on us."

"Great," I went on, "you have someone to talk to—me! But I don't. At least let me talk to someone."

"Okay," he said, "but not someone who knows us."

I found out that secretly married priests had been around Europe for a long time. In fact, two priests specialized in ministering with married priests—one a Sulpician, one a Jesuit. I chose the Jesuit, and he came down from Brussels to meet me. We sat in a small room in a Jesuit house in Paris. I told him my concerns, especially about scandal. He sat back from the table. "You Americans," he said. "You are so young in the church. Don't worry about the church; it can handle another scandal. What is important here is your friendship with this man!"

Immediately, the cloak of church law fell from my shoulder with a clunk on the floor. I sat forward, stunned. "Thank you," I said. "I just never saw it that way before—but, yes, friendship is much more important than church law." Later, when their first son was born, they asked me to baptize him, and I did.

As I spin on God's wheel in my eighty-second year on this planet, no biblical text means more to me than Isaiah 64:8 (ESV):

But now, O Lord, you are our Father;

We are the clay, and You are the Potter;

We are all the work of Your hand.

God's Divinity and Human Dignity Are Indivisible

Rabbi Dr. Israel Zoberman

As a congregational rabbi, I am called upon and privileged to emulate God's role as the supreme shepherd-pastor-healer, reaching out to lovingly care for my human flock, which is, I believe, at the heart of my rabbinic ministry and touches my multifaceted responsibilities. As an ordained clergyperson, I represent—with all its challenging complexities—God and the divine values of care, compassion, and concern, mindful that we all, congregants and human pastors, ultimately belong to God's congregation. Rabbi Abraham J. Heschel shares, "What constitutes being human, personhood? The ability to be concerned for other human beings. Animals are concerned for their own instinctive needs; the degree of our being human stands in direct proportion to the degree in which we care for others."[14]

In the Hebrew Scriptures, we read, "And God created man in His image ..."[15] It is this endowment of divinity upon human beings, linking them directly to the Creator, which endows them with divine dignity. In this spirit of protecting all human beings and not only kings,

---

[14] Abraham Joshua Heschel, "The Patient as a Person" in *The Insecurity of Freedom* (New York: Schocken Books,1972), 26.
[15] The Bible (Philadelphia: The Jewish Publication Society, 2000), Gen. 1:27.

as had been the case in the ancient world, the Talmud's rabbis teach us that "Whoever destroys a soul, it is considered as if he destroyed an entire world. And whoever saves a life, is considered as if he saved an entire world."[16] Judaism incorporates human caring and compassionate ways into the realm of religious obligations.

Relating helpfully and meaningfully to our fellow human beings is not to be left to one's whims, fulfilling the biblical commandment, "Love your fellow as yourself: I am the Lord."[17] Our love toward God is expressed through our love for God's creatures. Rabbi Akiva said, "Love your neighbor as yourself is the supreme principle of the Torah. You must not say, since I've been put to shame (by a fellow man), let him be put to shame; since I have been slighted, let him be slighted. Said Rabbi Tanhuna: 'If you do so, know whom you put to shame, for in the likeness of God made he him.'"[18]

God's creative charge, "Let there be light,"[19] reflects the divine will to bestow positive purpose and ultimate meaning upon creation, unlike the gods of the Gilgamesh epic, who create the world out of boredom and loneliness and choose to destroy it when they tire of their toy. God's

---

[16] Babylonian Talmud, Tractate Sanhedrin 4:5.

[17] Lev. 19:18 ESV.

[18] Tractate Pesahim 75a.

[19] Gen. 1:3 ESV.

creation receives the final divine enthusiastic approval, "And God saw all that He had, and found it very good."[20] Humanity is brought into a supportive environment attesting to God's benevolence. Human life is the finale of God's awesome gift, creation's crowning glory. We are entrusted with a sacred responsibility to safeguard the treasures of life. The granted human capacity for responsible behavior is an essential ingredient for loving care.

Creation is joined by redemption and revelation in God's encounter with Israel and humanity. When Israel finds itself under the debilitating yoke of Egyptian slavery, it is not forsaken by God. The rabbis tell us that when Israel suffers in exile, God's in-dwelling presence (the Shechinah) accompanies them and suffers along with them. God redeems the children of Israel from Egypt with the help of the people themselves. Their leaders, Moses and Aaron, although prompted by God to lead and act, need to mobilize the people and rally them around the common cause. Israel's dramatic redemption from Egypt became the leitmotif of rabbinic theology. Ultimately, human suffering is temporary, and God is bound to intervene and redeem. God's loving care for Israel is bound up with the messianic goal of humankind's redemption. We are all God's children.

Philosopher Martin Buber points out that "the perception of revelation is the basis for perceiving creation and redemption."[21] The highlight of God's revelation is expressed in the Sinaitic Covenant. At Mt. Sinai, the people of Israel pledge allegiance to the divine legislation. The gift of physical freedom from Pharaoh's house of bondage is augmented with the gift of spiritual freedom as well as responsibility through God's gift of Torah. Revelation is bound up to God's abundant love. "The question of why does God give this ability to man—why, at certain moments in the course of history, does He raise happenings and events from the level of the routine and the ordinary to that of Revelation—can only be answered by a reference to God's love. 'With everlasting love hast Thou loved the House of Israel, Thy people,'

---

[20] Gen. 1:31 GNV.
[21] Martin Buber, "The Men of Today and the Jewish Bible," *Israel Today*, 99.

says the Jew in his daily evening service, 'Torah and commandments, statutes and judgments has Thou taught us.'"[22]

The attitude of Jewish theology toward the relationship between God and Israel is multidimensional, stressing positive and negative aspects, joys as well as pains. Yet within that complex framework is a clear thrust reflecting God's caring nearness to Israel and humankind. Judaism has chosen to accent the human ability to overcome despair, transcending the difficulties of the present with a view toward a promising future. "For in our tradition, celebration of life is more important than mourning over the dead. When a wedding procession encounters a funeral procession in the street, the mourners must halt to allow the wedding party to proceed. Surely you know what respect we show our dead, but a wedding, symbol of life and renewal, symbol of promise, too, takes precedence. Our tradition orders us to affirm life and proclaim hope always. Shabbat interrupts all mourning, being as it is the embodiment of man's hope and his capacity for joy."[23]

The most trying experience between God and Israel during modern times and perhaps ever was the Holocaust, the destruction of one third of the Jewish people during World War II. That traumatic tragedy along with the joyful creation of the State of Israel in 1948 have shaped modern Jewish consciousness. Given the enormity of the Holocaust, it elicited a powerful contradictory response to the Jewish faith; some survivors lost it while others drew closer to it. Surely the Holocaust presents an ongoing theological challenge. Eli Wiesel, himself a Holocaust survivor, calls against despair and for an affirmation of the Jewish faith in spite of the destructive implications of the Holocaust, which he regards in stark, absolute terms as, "Auschwitz is the death of time, the end of creation."[24]

He consoles us with the following challenging proposition: "And yet, and yet … We went on believing, hoping, invoking His name. In the endless engagement with God, we proved to Him that we were more patient than He, more compassionate too. In other words, we did not

---

[22] Jacob J. Petuchowski, *Ever Since Sinai* (New York: Scribe Publications, 1968), 40.
[23] Elie Weisel, *A Jew Today* (New York: Random House, 1978), 163.
[24] Ibid., 198.

give up on Him either. For this is the essence of being Jewish: never to give up—never to yield to despair." [25] The State of Israel represents the Jewish people's promised and promising rebirth and, in a way, even collective resurrection.

I subscribe to the Buberian "I and Thou" relationship model reflecting a meaningful human encounter that attempts to bring out depth experiences from the involved parties that elicit caring and responsible humane responsiveness. "All real living is meeting"[26]—a genuine meeting between human beings and between them and God (the two meetings being interrelated) provides for a mode of living characterized by mutual acknowledgement and respect, inner growth and self-actualization.

The desired encounter is a sharing that overcomes inhibitions and hesitations, willingly risking with the understanding that the sharing is mutual and acceptance is ever-present. The encounter with another person thus becomes a key to building our own identity, nourishing and shaping it. "Through Thou a man becomes I."[27]

The meaning of such a human encounter became poignantly evident to me within the creative context of clinical pastoral education (CPE). "The modern clinical pastoral training program has provided many seminary students and clergymen with opportunities to explore levels of depth in human experience. In hospitals, prisons, and clinics, pastors have 'read the human documents' and, in so doing, have found a perspective of depth in their work."[28]

Following my ordination as a reform rabbi from the Hebrew Union College–Jewish Institute of Religion, Cincinnati campus, in 1974, I was fortunate indeed to take four units (two advanced) of CPE during the three years in which I served at Temple Judah in Cedar Rapids, Iowa (1974–1977), leading to my becoming a clinical member in the Association for Clinical Pastoral Education (ACPE). My training took

[25] Ibid., 164.
[26] Martin Buber, *I and Thou* (New York: Scribner Library, 2nd ed., 1958), 11.
[27] Ibid., 28.
[28] Thomas W. Klink, *Depth Perspectives in Pastoral Work* (New Jersey: Prentice- Hall, 1965), 18.

place at St. Luke's Methodist Hospital, with the ACPE Supervisor, the Rev. Dr. Russell Stiffer. I am probably one of the first rabbis to receive CPE training. My case study (verbatim reports) evolved from the congregation I served as well as the hospital setting. I visited with patients from a variety of faith groups and denominations who were hospitalized in various departments.

I had special exposure to psychiatric patients during two CPE units at both the closed and open psychiatric wards. I acquired tools from the behavioral sciences, enabling me to better communicate with people and attend to their needs. I have become more conscientious of people's needs through verbal and nonverbal communication. I have gained a deeper level of sensitivity to the encounter with fellow human beings, whether they are patients in the hospital, congregants at my temple, fellow CPE students, or people in general.

Through my CPE training, I have become less inhibited to enter a relationship with therapeutic dimensions; in fact, I willingly explore the possibilities for such an encounter with the knowledge that I can be of help to people and that it is my responsibility to actively pursue it depending, of course, on the circumstances.

This mode of relating to people is turning the Buberian "I and Thou" model into a beneficial living reality. It is the willingness to go beyond the surface of human relationships, exposing our inner selves—caution is advised though when interacting with congregants—to one another and recognizing that intimate sharing of self, while painful at times, ultimately may promote self-growth and a higher sense of wholeness. When we reach into ourselves, we gain new insights into our unique being and life becomes ever more meaningful. "Depth, of personal meaning, is derived from the unique and individual mass of memories, values, experiences against which every person measures and weighs new communications and events."[29] Self-exploration of depth experience is a vital link in grasping the fullness of others. Appreciation for our individual uniqueness leads us to appreciate the unique depth of our fellow humans.

---

[29] Klink, 18.

While serving Temple Israel in Gary, Indiana (1977–1981), I became the first rabbi to earn the doctorate of ministry (in pastoral care and counseling) from the McCormick Theological Seminary (affiliated with the Presbyterian Church, USA) in Chicago in 1980. Jewish seminaries, including my own, began offering a doctor of ministry degree much later. I will always cherish my depth sharing with fellow CPE and doctor of ministry students, each of us unique in our own individuality and theological tradition. Encountering one another out of our own contexts of reference, we gained new insights into our precious differences and commonalities. Particularly in the CPE setting, the encounter at times lacked spontaneity due to being "arranged," and at times the participants went overboard trying to find fault with others. An intimate encounter ought not to be a license to hurt others. However, we are enabled to open up and be free of conventional inhibitions.

During my tenure at Temple B'rith Sholom in Springfield, Illinois (1982–1985), I worked with Dr. Richard L. Dayringer and Dr. Glen W. Davidson, who were professors at the Department of Medical Humanities at Southern Illinois University School of Medicine. I also became a certified pastoral counselor in the American Association of Pastoral Counselors (AAPC).

Restoring human wholeness is enabled through the respective religious traditions that clergypersons represent. "I believe that problem-laden persons who seek help from a pastor do so for very deep reasons— from the desire to look at ourselves in a theological perspective,"[30] is the message of Dr. Paul W. Pruyser. The pastor is in an enviable position to function within both theological and behavioral frames of reference. "The modern pastor must represent transcendent values to persons who live in settings untouched by traditional controls."[31] The religious community as a whole can play a constructive role in transforming lonely lives untouched by transcendent values into lives with a sense of attachment to both a higher purpose and a caring community.

---

[30] Paul W. Pruyser, *The Minister as Diagnostician* (Philadelphia: The Westminster Press, 1976), 43.
[31] Ibid., 65.

I view my pastoral role as one which is not limited to an encounter in my study's privacy, rather as one infusing my various functions in the congregation: visiting the sick, officiating at life-cycle events, preaching, educating, administering, promoting interfaith dialogue, community involvement, socializing, and all services in the context of my ministry, which is quite broad. Dr. Pruyser sets up a pastoral model that responds to my own vision that I have tried to practice for over four decades—a model of a pastor reaching out in caring love to the community one serves. It is indeed a sacred charge and the high privilege to be deeply involved in the lives of the people we serve and lead; facilitating their growth and our own; helping them to respond to life's challenging realities; and sharing intimately precious doubts and agonies, uncertain searches, and joyful exaltations in the bonding love of eternal values.

> But I toy with a picture, a picture of a pastor who goes out and loves. He will visit in people's homes to demonstrate and nurture compassion. He will seek communion in his counseling, he will try to embed in communion the sick, bereft, poor, imprisoned and oppressed. And he will assume that the people he meets, the people who seek him out, the people who knock at his office door, or who call him at home late at night, are essentially seeking acceptance in a community of love.... They want to love and be loved, and they want to know what love is, by engagements with their pastors in the fellowship of their church.[32]

As a son of Polish Holocaust survivors who was born in Chu, Kazakhstan, in 1945 and spent his early childhood in displaced persons camps in Austria and Germany, I am particularly attached to Dr. Viktor E. Frankl and his school of logotherapy, though I am generally eclectic in my psychotherapeutic approach and leaning toward the client-centered Rogerian model that works well with logotherapy. Dr.

---

[32] Ibid., 66.

Frankl served as professor of psychiatry and neurology at the University of Vienna Medical School. He was imprisoned in concentration camps by the Nazis and lost his wife, parents, and brother. Professor Gordon Allport, a Harvard psychologist, teaches us, "How could he—every possession lost, every value destroyed, suffering from hunger, cold and brutality, hourly expecting extermination—how could he find life worth preserving? A psychiatrist who personally has faced such extremity is a psychiatrist worth listening to. He, if anyone, should be able to view our human condition wisely and with compassion."[33]

Dr. Frankl emerged from the terrifying crucible of the concentration camps experience with logotherapy, the third Viennese school of psychotherapy, which is therapy provided through the search and discovery of meaning in one's life, emphasizing the spiritual dimension. It followed Freud's school of psychoanalysis (emphasizing the unconscious, striving for pleasure, unresolved early conflicts) and Adler's school of individual psychology (striving for power). Three basic concepts compose logotherapy: (1) the freedom of will; (2) the will to meaning; and (3) the meaning of life. However, the second concept, the will to meaning, is the central one.

Thus, Freud's will to pleasure and Adler's will to power are augmented by Frankl's will to meaning. Dr. Frankl lost a manuscript of his, ready for publication, while incarcerated. The loss of his "spiritual child" presented him with an agonizing existential dilemma. He was confronted with his central question of life's meaning in the face of likely having neither a physical child nor a spiritual one to survive him. However, he was able to overcome his despair through his hope to write his manuscript again. His attempt to reconstruct the confiscated work while surrounded with the ever-present threat of death gave him the strength of spirit and body to endure the suffering.

The inmates in the concentration camps who could find meaning in their lives through the entertaining of goals to be accomplished, as in rewriting Dr. Frankl's lost book, or the thoughtful contemplation of loved ones, were more likely to survive than those inmates who could

---

[33] Victor E. Frankl, *Man's Search for Meaning* (New York: Pocket Books, 1974), viii.

discover no meaning in their dreadful existence. My father, Yechiel Zoberman, while serving in the Red Army during World War II, hid in his boot a photo of his family, which was risky were he to be captured by the Germans. Meaning discovered and pondered upon provides a dimension of hope to survive the worst of conditions. Beyond mere physical survival, important as it is, a debilitating environment, such as that of a concentration camp, presents the unfortunate victims with a challenge through which their lives could be ennobled. Those who chose to share their meager bread with others and helped their fellows while risking their own lives revealed the dignity of the human spirit, not allowing the sacred spark within them to extinguish.

Despair in the framework of logotherapy is not in itself an alarming mental condition; rather it is a uniquely human characteristic. "They should know that despair over the apparent meaninglessness of life constitutes a human achievement rather than a neurosis."[34] Despair over meaning in one's life, according to Dr. Frankl, is only a temporary condition. With patience, one is capable of discerning meaning. Mental health is conceived in logotherapy as "noodynamics," a degree of tension between two poles—one representing a meaning to be fulfilled and the other, the person who has the responsibility to fulfill it.

Dr. Frankl thus denies the traditional view that mental well-being depends on a homeostatic condition that by definition precludes tension. Rather, it assumes that a state of tension is indispensable for the human search for meaning, with the potential to restore one's mental health and maintain it. "What man actually needs is not a tensionless state but rather the striving and struggling for some goal worthy of him."[35] He makes the point that in the case of neurotic individuals, the need for challenge in one's attempt to identify meaning in life is even more crucial than in an ordinary situation. Consequently, the increase of tension between a person and the awaiting goals creates a greater awareness of the task at hand, serving a beneficial therapeutic function.

Each person has one's own meaning in life that waits to be

---

[34] Victor E. Frankl, *The Unconscious God* (New York: Simon and Schuster, 1975), 139.
[35] Frankl, *Man's Search for Meaning*, 166.

fulfilled, a meaning that has its own unique context. The role of the logotherapist is to raise in the client an awareness of the potential meaningful possibilities to be realized. "The logotherapist's role consists in widening and broadening the visual field of the patient so that the whole spectrum of meaning and values becomes visible to him."[36] The client has the responsibility to respond to life's challenge and adapt meanings and values that cannot be imposed by anyone else, including the logotherapist.

Dr. Frankl has high praise for the potential role of religion in human life. The guidelines mapped out in one's religion are of great therapeutic value, presenting a formidable frame of reference for facing life's vicissitudes. "Religion provides man with a spiritual anchor, with a feeling of security such as he can find nowhere else."[37] He shares that inmates in concentration camps who attempted to preserve their religion in thought and act, as much as was humanly possible in the inhumane environment, found a unique source of strength and inspiration to rely upon.

Underlying logotherapy is an unconditional faith and unconditional meaning, the hallmark of which is the indomitable human spirit of hope in the face of a despairing reality, a trust that ultimately God and life will not betray. Dr. Frankl presents the prophet Habakkuk as a model for the invincibility of the human spirit. In spite and because of the dire economic conditions that the biblical prophet and his people faced, he praised and rejoiced in God. Habakkuk did not give up in resignation but chose to affirm his ultimate faith and trust in the ultimate goodness of God and life. "Although the fig tree shall not blossom, neither shall fruit be in the vines; the labor of the olive shall fail, and the fields shall yield no meat; the flock shall be cut off from the fold, and there shall be no herd in the stall. Yet I will rejoice in the Lord, I will joy in the God of my salvation."[38]

It was the same unconditional trust in unconditional meaning that

---

[36] Frankl, *Man's Search for Meaning*, 166.
[37] Ibid., 174.
[38] Quoted in Frankl, *The Will to Meaning*, 157.

23

preserved Dr. Frankl's life in the concentration camps. He was able to overcome the trauma of losing his "spiritual child," the manuscript that was confiscated from him, by realizing that life's meaningfulness could not depend on haphazard events for life to be meaningful. If life was meaningful, it would be so disregarding changing conditions and circumstances. "But after wrestling with my despair for hours, shivering from typhus fever I finally asked myself what sort of meaning could depend on whether or not a manuscript of mine is printed. I would not really care. But if there is meaning, it is unconditional meaning, and neither suffering nor dying can detract from it."[39]

It is indeed the attitude of the Jewish faith that Dr. Frankl brings forth in his spiritual psychotherapeutic system. Judaism asserts the eternal value of the human spirit that even death itself cannot bury. The God of life is higher than the God of death. It speaks of faith that acknowledges the ultimate goodness of life while facing the most discouraging reality; it praises God, who stands for hope and renewal when the chips are down and the natural human inclination is to deny God. It affirms the uniqueness of each human life and its infinite dignity, that God's divinity and human dignity are inseparable, and that we are given the freedom of choice along with a charge and a capacity for a responsible and hallowed way of life—the oneness of God and humanity.

Reflecting upon the nature of modern society, Dr. Frankl coined the term "the existential vacuum." With the abandonment of long-established traditions and the failure to replace them with new ones, along with the hovering threat of total annihilation, one experiences an overwhelming sense of meaninglessness and emptiness, contributing to alienation. This spiritless trend has been affected by teachings that bring forth a negative message of human futility, breeding passivity toward life, and quenching human self-awe, as well as awe at the world. The outcome of such a perverse philosophy is the destruction of positive human beings and of humanity itself, figuratively and literally. "I am absolutely convinced that the gas chambers of Auschwitz, Treblinka,

---

[39] Ibid., 156.

and Maidenek were ultimately prepared not in some ministry or other in Berlin, but rather at the desks and in the lecture halls of nihilistic scientists and philosophers."[40]

Dr. Frankl postulates three avenues for endowing one's life with meaning: (1) creative values—achieving tasks that we set up; (2) experiential values—experiencing The Good, The True, The Beautiful, or by experiencing one human being as unique through love; and (3) attitudinal values—how we approach and respond to suffering, which "is the highest achievement to man."[41] Utilizing attitudinal values as a means in one's search for therapeutic meaning is of special value to the clergyperson in responding to the personal agony and depth of despair of the people we serve.

Suffering, being a fixed component in human life from which none of us can escape, is potentially a challenge of the highest order, according to Dr. Frankl. Through our attempt to instill meaningfulness in our lives, suffering, when imposed upon us, rather than merely robbing us of joy and satisfaction, may serve as a catalyst for human fulfillment. Suffering in whatever mode, whether in a terminal illness, the loss of a loved one, or a sense of alienation, can become a gateway for human growth. Confronting the miseries we face, with a thought-through response entailing human dignity and courage, enables us to face life meaningfully in our own eyes and in the eyes of those around us.

Dr. Frankl shares with us the case of a nurse in his department who suffered from inoperable cancer. Her despair was rooted in her inability to work, for her love toward her profession was her life's central force. His approach was to tell her that working a number of hours a day can be achieved by many, but to be in her condition while overcoming despair would be a real triumph. Dr. Frankl also pointed out to the anguished nurse that she would be unfair to all the sick people she had treated if she herself acted as if a terminally ill person's life were without meaning.

Rabbi Harold M. Schulweis, who was the spiritual leader of

---

[40] Victor E. Frankl, *The Doctor and the Soul*, (New York: Vintage Books, 1973), xxi.
[41] Ibid., xiii.

Congregation Valley Beth Sholom in Encino, California, attempted to revitalize the contemporary synagogue in the midst of a complex environment with the emphasis on profound caring, merging the Jew's life-cycle events with a responsive congregational setting, thus bonding more intimately the Jew to the religious community.

> The synagogue today is challenged by the secular religions to create a community of personal concern centered around the mitzvoth (commandments) of every Jew's life passage. In an age of loneliness, the synagogue has a golden opportunity to make of Jewish rites of passage the consequence, the celebrating outcome of Jewish activity. Jewish activity in which Jews as Jews help Jews through the normal crises which attend the stages of personal and family growth. The man in the Jew and the Jew in the man needs a compassionate ear, a responsive spirit, an informed intelligence in which to confide.[42]

I myself have attempted to link my congregants to their religious heritage and communal belonging by celebrating highlights of their human and Jewish journey in the context of the Sabbath experience—special birthdays, anniversaries, professional milestones, and accomplishments included.

During my tenure as associate rabbi at Ohef Sholom Temple in Norfolk, Virginia (1981–1982), and since 1985 as founding rabbi of Congregation Beth Chaverim in Virginia Beach, Virginia, I have participated in an interfaith spiritual panel at Lee's Friends, which assists cancer survivors. I have also affiliated with Jewish Family Service of Tidewater, serving on its board of directors, as well as chairing the Hospice Committee. I am a founding member of the Professional Advisory Group at the School of CPE at Sentara Hospitals with ACPE Supervisor, the Rev. Dr. Russell H. Davis and his successor ACPE

---

[42] Harold M. Schulweis, "The Challenge of the New Secular Religions," *Conservative Judaism* 30, no. 3 (1979): 14.

Supervisor, the Rev. Dr. Uwe C. Scharf. I have spoken to the CPE students on Judaism and health.

My Congregation Beth Chaverim met for its first three years (1982–1985) at Wesleyan Acres United Methodist Church in Virginia Beach. The next ten years (1985–1995), we were at the Catholic Church of the Ascension in Virginia Beach. Currently Congregation Beth Chaverim is home to two African American churches, New Jerusalem Ministries, and Emanuel Way of the Cross Church. For sixteen years, we have had a joint Thanksgiving Eve service with Eastern Shore Chapel Episcopal Church in Virginia Beach. At the 2016 service, the church's rector, The Rev. Thomas Deppe, bestowed on me the title, "Honorary Senior Rabbi Scholar." I am past national interfaith chair for The Jewish Council for Public Affairs (JCPA).

A Call to Service

Imam Mohamed Magid
"And We have not sent you, [O Muhammad]
but as a mercy to the worlds." 21:107

Counseling was a regular practice of the Prophet Muhammad, the last and final prophet of God. Muslims strive to follow the example of the Prophet Muhammad. As the son of a leading religious scholar in Sudan, I too learned at a very young age the importance of consciously selecting this individual as the role model to guide the decisions I would make throughout my life. The above verse from the Qur'an has been particularly influential in the development of my role as a spiritual counselor. The Prophet Muhammad, may the peace and blessings of God be upon him, was a man of mercy. His interactions with others epitomized mercy, the words he spoke taught mercy to others, and the way he lived exemplified the importance and benefit of creating a merciful community.

> "In most of their secret talks there is no good; but if one exhorts to a deed of charity or justice or conciliation between men, (secrecy is permissible): to him who does this, seeking the good pleasure of Allah, We shall soon give reward of the highest value." 4:114

The Prophet Muhammad, may the peace and blessings of God be upon him, was the best example of a counselor. He was known to be a devoted listener. He listened to those who wanted to speak to him, he spoke to those who sought his advice, and in his ever-loving character he reached out to those who needed help but hesitated to ask. When someone spoke to him or he was speaking to someone, he would turn his entire body to face them completely, letting them know that they had his undivided attention. He was a man of deep compassion and had a unique ability to connect with people of all backgrounds. Though he was a prophet of God, he spoke with everyone, even attending to children when they spoke to him or played with him. I often reflect on the famous story of the Prophet Muhammad in which he noticed a man sitting alone in the mosque. It was not time for any of the congregational prayers, so he approached the man and inquired about his well-being. The man explained to the Prophet, though hesitant to "complain" to him, that he was facing financial difficulty and was worried about his situation. The Prophet taught him a prayer: "O God! I seek Your protection from worry and grief, and I seek Your protection from weakness and laziness, and I seek Your protection from miserliness and cowardice, and I seek Your protection from burden of debt and anger of men."

The Prophet provided the prescription, and the man left feeling empowered. There are numerous supplications the Prophet left behind. The Qur'an itself is counseling to the Prophet, may the peace and blessings of God be upon him: "We do indeed know how thy heart is distressed at what they say. But celebrate the praises of your Lord and be of those who prostrate themselves and serve your Lord until there come onto you the Hour that is Certain" (15:97–98).

God is reminding the Prophet that regardless of what is upon Him, God is his support. God will never forsake His servant, and He is the one who is ultimately in control. For any situation, you will find a prayer of comfort in the Qur'an or in the traditions of the Prophet. I believe this is one of my greatest tools in counseling. I strive to provide as much emotional support and inspiration as I am able, but as an Imam and a counselor, I know well the power of reconnecting individuals with our Creator, our provider. All things are in the hands of God and we as counselors, particularly religious or spiritual counselors, are a means for these individuals to reestablish or strengthen the link to the One in whose hands lies power over all things.

As a child, and well into my youth, I observed my father interact with others. His manner was always that of humility, sincerity, and compassion. While he shouldered the many responsibilities of his position, he always found time to attend to those who needed his guidance or advice. He always wore a smile. People were drawn to his warmth and his kindheartedness. He could shake a man's hand in greeting him and by the time they went their separate ways, he may have learned about the man's family, his hopes, and his challenges. Whenever people left him, they left with a sense of encouragement. I knew that each time he did this, he was modeling the example of the same man he had always reminded me to model, the Prophet Muhammad, may the peace and blessings of God be upon him. As I became older and began teaching in the small town in which we lived, I noticed that more and more that people would approach me with questions, and over time, those evolved into presenting problems or concerns of the home, within the family, and even in faith. Very soon, I found myself answering similar questions to those that my father was hearing from others.

Through observing him, I learned to handle each person's concerns as a trust. He heard countless stories of people's personal struggles, yet he never looked down on anyone and he respected the sacredness of what they shared, being careful to never break the trust they put in him. People were opening up to me, revealing something of their hearts, and I had to honor that. I learned I had to separate the people from their actions and in some cases to dislike the actions I would hear about, but I could never to allow those to define my view of the heart of the individual. There is good in every person, and we must always strive to bring that out. When I would see my father mediating conflict between families, his patience never wavered. He spent time with them working through the frustrations, diligently trying to find the source from where it all stemmed. Here in the United States, the needs of the community sometimes outweigh the resources we have available. Imams have to partner with professional counselors to provide the religious aspect but allow the professionals to take the time, week to week, to sit with individuals, couples, and families to fully address the problems they are facing. This allows people the time to become more aware of themselves, the basis of their actions and speech, and the consequences of their decisions.

My father's commitment to helping those around him was genuine. I would see him pray before and after he counseled. He prayed for guidance and for God's help for those who came to him. My father knew he was merely an instrument in God's divine plan. The ultimate change comes from God, and we continuously pray for those in need. We pray that He guides each of our hearts, our tongues, and our actions in a way that brings us closer to Him and allows us to be recipients of His divine love and mercy.

While my father modeled for me life as a teacher and scholar, my grandfather showed me what it meant to be an activist. He often took time to get to know the poor families in his village and spent time with the most vulnerable people, getting to know them when others did not feel they were worthy of their time. It was through him that I gained a sense of what it looked like to reach out to others. In my teenage years, I volunteered with the United Nations in Sudan, and my team was called upon to help refugees relocating from western Sudan to Khartoum. Thrilled to be doing my part to help others, bright eyed and with a smile on my face, I enthusiastically collected material to distribute around the camp. As I was doing so, I saw a lady in the distance holding a small child. As I approached her, I could see the distress on her face. She was clearly famished. I could see the bones in her face and hands—she had not had sufficient food in quite some time. *Praise be to God*, I thought. *I am here now, and I can deliver the food she needs."* "Son, you are too late. The child has died," she said. She held the tiny, lifeless body in her arms. My heart dropped; I was too late. This experience shook me to my core. I remember it frequently, particularly in my advocacy work. Help cannot be delayed. In this instance, it was food. In another instance, it might be an emotional crisis or a crisis of faith. We need to connect material with the spiritual care of individuals to make sure that whomever we are helping is in a good place in mind, body, and soul. Rather than "Feed the Homeless," we should eat *with* the homeless and know their stories and their struggles to empower them to face their challenges with strength. It was through these experiences that I began to see counseling as a means of serving God.

My traditional training in Sudan unquestionably provided me a strong foundation upon which to start a life of service to others. However, after moving to America and becoming an Imam to a very diverse community, I quickly discovered that there was an array of new challenges about which I needed to learn. Muslim Americans live in a multicultural and multiethnic society. There is diversity within our theology; there are born Muslims and Muslim converts from all walks of life. Young American Muslims were grappling with issues that I never had to face as a young man growing up in Sudan. There were immigrants who came for opportunity, and there were immigrants who came fleeing their war-torn homelands with little more than the shirts on their backs. I very quickly understood that my traditional training would now require supplemental training to provide appropriate guidance to people experiencing something so different than what I had previously encountered. In dealing with scenarios that people were facing, I realized how much they were entrusting me with their quandaries. As a patient goes to a doctor looking for a cure to a physical ailment, they were looking to me for a cure for their personal struggles. The individuals who sat in front of me were inviting me into their private emotional space. I realized then that counseling is one of the most important relationships an Imam will have with his congregants— helping them to alleviate their pain and providing comfort and hope in moving forward. I decided to enroll in a psychology class at the local university in the United States. I tried to actively learn about American society and its priorities, its strengths, and its challenges. I needed all of this insight to help me begin to see the world from the perspective of those coming to me.

Additionally, this realization of the gap between my traditional training and secondary training highlighted the importance of addressing counseling themes as large-scale community-level preventive methods. Religious leaders should work in partnership with specialized professionals in addressing community issues before they arise, utilizing sermons, town halls, and educational programs to address community needs at all age levels. In my experience over the years, such opportunities have created openings for individuals to approach me more easily on the topics presented. Recently, we have had a completely new phenomenon of social media and virtual societies in which people live alternate lives. This is a challenge that is new to everyone and has some impact on the vast majority of people living in the United States today. It requires partnering with youth counselors and leaders, as they are better able to connect with the youth. Religious leaders and counselors need to work with community leaders to holistically approach the faith, spirituality, and mental health of the community.

As an Imam, I also understand the importance of self-care for all the mental health and spiritual care givers of our communities. You have to take care of yourself before you can take care of others. In counseling, you are meeting people at different stages of life. Perhaps someone is coming for premarital counseling as he or she starts a new life with another, and on the same day another may come grieving the loss of a parent or of a child. In any of these cases, you open yourself up to receiving information about their joy or their suffering. My responsibility is to provide support and comfort during their time of need. As counselors, we must balance being compassionate and caring about the person's well-being with maintaining a degree of separation. It is important not to become absorbed by the problems presented, as doing so would inevitably impact your own personal life and relationships. Furthermore, as a counselor for a religious community, you see the same individuals who sought counseling from you in social gatherings within the congregation with spouses, children, and friends. It is critical to ensure that the dignity of any person is not compromised by a breach of confidentiality and that our own views of that person are not tainted or distorted by what was shared of their vulnerabilities or weaknesses. Our roles within the congregation demand that we exercise these behaviors every day with numerous people at one time. Therefore, there is less separation than a professional counselor may have, and that requires extra attention be given to one's self to ensure a healthy work-life balance.

The Prophet Muhammad, may the peace and blessings of God be upon him, frequently took solitary retreats to reflect on the state of the community. This is a practice I utilize myself for spiritual meditation and remembrance of God. This time of quiet allows me to clear my mind, reflect, and reenergize to return and continue to support the community. It is my hope that clergy of all faiths may come together to share experiences on common issues and best practices.

In conclusion, counseling others helps you understand your own vulnerabilities as a human being, thereby bringing out humility and understanding of oneself. If done correctly, reflecting on the challenges of others strengthens our compassion and care for those around us. When all is said and done, it is the satisfaction and contentment of pleasing God that is the true measure of success. In return, He provides you the spiritual satisfaction and comfort that you need. The insight gained as a result of counseling decreases the tendency to pass judgment on others. I am often reminded of Rumi's famous line of poetry, which says, "Beyond right and wrong there is a field, meet me there." Counseling is a way of seeking the spiritual space where all people can meet, regardless of any challenges that set us apart.

The Strong Drink of Friendship

Jay Bergstresser

Give strong drink to one who is perishing,
and wine to those in bitter distress;
let them drink and forget their poverty,
and remember their misery no more.
—Proverbs 31:6–7 (NIV)

Occasionally, a wise-cracking homeless person will tell me that the above passage is his favorite Bible verse. We've discovered in our monthly outreach to the homeless on the streets of Cocoa Beach, Florida, that the "strong drink" they really need is friendship.

For thirteen years, I served as pastor of a typical sleepy Christian congregation. We showed up for worship on Sunday and to the occasional choir practice or committee meeting during the week. Other than that, there wasn't much happening. We were big into worship and church administration. I remember preaching sermons on how being a Christian meant following Christ in "real" ways, by helping the poor with their immediate needs for food and shelter. I preached those sermons year after year. Then someone woke up from her sermon-induced coma and took me seriously.

She was the most unlikely candidate for the job of social ministry angel of mercy. She was a very real person: hard-baked and rough around the edges, a working-class gal from Toledo, Ohio. Need I say more? Looking back now, Sari was perhaps the perfect person to take on this work with the "least of these." She understood their world, spoke their language, and wouldn't take anything from anyone. It all began with a food closet, probably smaller than the walk-in closet in your home. Somehow, she fed hundreds out of there.

In the beginning, it was just brown paper bags of groceries given with little fanfare and less fraternizing. The needy were provided with those bags of food, sure, but they were hungry when they got there. Volunteers started brewing pots of coffee and bringing in bagels, bananas, and frozen waffles. Soon, a regular breakfast was being served in the adjacent fellowship hall, and a community was born. Many who came for help had cars, but some came on foot. Sari put out the call for mechanics to fix up and distribute bikes to those who couldn't afford a car or had lost their licenses. Free bikes were soon being prepped and given out to tears of joy and appreciation.

Then it was my turn.

I wish I could say it was a revelation from heaven, a word from the "Big Guy" himself, but it was my hyperactive Lutheran conscience. There is nothing as annoying as a nagging conscience. Here's what happened. One day on my way to the church, I noticed a woman slumped in a bus shelter outside a grocery store. She looked miserable and desperate, and it broke my heart. I swallowed hard and kept driving. The next morning, she was there again. Same cowardice from me—I did *nothing*.

I felt like a phony. "Help the poor, comfort the grieving," I had sermonized so many times to my parishioners. So much for practicing what you preach! Luckily, God had another plan for me. He put a pro in my path. Pastor Dave was a winter visitor each year here in Florida (folks commonly known as snowbirds). He had worked with the homeless and the addicted for years up north, and he was gracious enough to train me and several others to reach out to the homeless on the streets.

Honestly, it was frightening at first. We had no idea what to expect. Would we be laughed at, cursed, attacked? We braced ourselves for the abuse and prepared for the worst. On the day of our first outing, we were filled with fear and foreboding. We stalled as long as we could before heading out.

If you think you already know what you're going to find when you reach out to the homeless, it just shows that you've never done it. Every encounter is surprising. You soon discover it's not about the supplies you've brought in your car or the help-line numbers you might have at your fingertips. It's about friendship, plain and simple. These encounters are holy encounters and have been some of the best experiences in my life—the most memorable and joy giving. They are also so much fun. Yeah, I wrote *fun*. I once described it like a cross between Christmas morning and ten cups of coffee. I'm not sure why that is, but my theory is that when you do something that Christ commands, his power flows through you, and it's a rush.

I realize that, in the past, when I used to drive by a homeless person, there was some sort of a veil over my eyes. I've only come to recognize that truth after seven years of doing street ministry. Sometimes the veil was placed there by my own prejudices and preconceived notions. Other times, it was some manifestation of the demons that have so many of our homeless friends entrapped: drugs, alcohol, and mental illness. When you finally "get out there" and have that one-to-one encounter, the spell is broken, the veil is brushed back, and you see the face of God.

Sound like a bold statement? Not really. Jesus promised that we would meet him in the "least of these." The funny thing is that, once you really get to know the homeless, you'll find friends. Some of the homeless in Cocoa Beach we've known now for seven years. They are our dear friends. Four, with our encouragement, have escaped the streets. We go out in search of new homeless friends, in teams of two, two Saturday mornings a month.

From time to time, we involve our youth in these helping ministries of our church, Resurrection.[43] We do this in an intentional way to show them that actively helping others is what it means to be a follower of Christ. Once, an overnight youth retreat had been scheduled at the church from Friday evening into Saturday morning. Youth from a number of different Lutheran churches in our area took part in this two-day program. On Friday, they walked out to the beach, played games, and watched movies. On Saturday morning, they would be involved with our helping ministries—waking up early, eating breakfast, and then participating in some aspect of the program.

On Friday night, before bed, they signed up for the area of our ministries that interested them. Some agreed to help pack food bags in the pantry, some would repair bikes in our bike shop, a few would work in the pantry garden preparing the ground for the fall planting, and the remaining teens would help cook and serve a pancake and sausage breakfast to our homeless friends and pantry clients later Saturday morning. Additionally, four of the most mature youth would be part of the Living Hope Street Outreach. That Saturday morning, three of our volunteers, whom I will call Ben, Emma, and Ann, and I sat with these four youth and instructed them in some of the basics of interacting with

---

[43] The following story is excerpted from my book, *Strong Drink for the Perishing: Transformative Outreach to the Homeless* (John J. Bergstresser, 2017).

the homeless in a positive way. Most importantly, we told them, was to show respect and to focus on the person being helped.

The four youth who wanted to go out were girls. Two of the girls went north with Ben and Ann, while the other two girls went with Emma and me to cover the southern part of our territory. We parked and walked in the direction of the popular local bar. Along the way, we passed a doorway where a homeless man, whom I knew to be Joe, was sprawled out in a very uncomfortable position. It was as if he had been in the late stages of playing the game Twister and had fallen. One arm was across his chest, and one leg was twisted behind. He was sprawled out and so drunk that he could not speak; only making barely recognizable grunts. The girls were shocked by the sight and instinctively drew back. I just walked up to him, crouched down, and said, "Hi, Joe, it's Pastor Jay."

He grunted something indistinguishable, not looking up.

I said, "You know, the church pantry opens in a little over an hour, and we'd love to see you there."

"Yeah," he mumbled. I reached over and took his hand. "Good to see you, Joe. We'll catch up with you back at the church."

"Okay," he moaned. As we walked away, I hoped the message to the girls was clear: we love people where they are. We try to understand and befriend. Maybe if Joe feels that genuine friendship enough, it might inspire him to enter drug rehab and get his life back on track.

As we turned the corner onto the side street toward the beach access, it was the girls' turn. Without being prompted, they walked up and spoke to a man who was seated on the curb. He had a large military backpack and had obviously spent many hours in the sun—his skin was a reddish brown, his lips chapped and cracked. His head was bowed when we approached, with a cigarette hanging from his lips. When he looked up, a tear was rolling down his cheek and he looked deeply depressed. When the girls started talking to him, he perked right up. They told him cheerfully that there would be a pancake breakfast in about an hour and that he was invited. What impressed me most was that their tone was so genuine, so caring.

He picked up on that too. He said his name was Ricky and that he would be there. While they were talking to Ricky, I was conversing with a man in a motorized wheelchair nearby who was one of our regulars at Resurrection's food pantry. I recognized him but had never learned his name because he wasn't homeless. He said he'd be there as well. When we finally left Ricky, he was a different person: smiling and positive. Just a few words, a little caring, changed his morning. No food or money was given—only friendship and an invitation to breakfast.

To our delight, Ricky did indeed come to breakfast that morning, and so did Joe, still drunk but in much better shape about an hour and a half later. When they arrived, they were the only two in the social hall to be served, so the other youth, with nothing else to do, sat at the round table with them. On breaks from their service that morning, the youth had been playing cards. There was now much laughter as Ricky and Joe, after eating, taught the kids how to play twenty-one. One of the adult leaders said, in a joking tone, "I'm not sure about this!"

"I am," I replied with a smile.

The interactions on the street and in the social hall were more than I had hoped for. These kids had made a real difference in just a couple of hours, but the best was yet to come.

The next morning, Ricky came to worship. Unlike most of the homeless, he didn't sit in the back row. He came right up the center aisle and sat next to one of our long-time female members. I was delighted to see her helping him set up his hymnal. She was smiling, pleasant, and welcoming. When it was time for Holy Communion, she came up to the rail, arm in arm with Ricky. She was bringing him forward. She showed him where to kneel and how we receive the Lord's Supper. Standing at the communion rail after he received communion, with a big smile on his face, he put one hand over his heart and thrust the other up toward the ceiling, pointing. He was looking up as the tears were rolling down. The funniest reaction was when the usher, standing at the head of the aisle, looked toward the ceiling where Ricky was pointing as if to ask, *Is there a leak?*

Such unbridled thanks and praise is not common for those of us raised in the Lutheran tradition. We're a pretty reserved bunch, but for a homeless man who had found food, love, and acceptance, he just couldn't help himself. I'm pretty sure of one thing: God was smiling.

Israel: Our Ancestral Homeland

Rabbi Ari J. Goldstein

I was born into the rabbi business. Being the son of a rabbi, I was well acquainted with family trips cut short and waiting patiently while my parents had long conversations in the grocery store with people I had never seen before.

There is one story I recall that my parents thoroughly dislike. In fact, I have learned not to tell this story in their presence because it makes them deeply uncomfortable. I recall one time when I was seven years old, I was asked to babysit my five-year-old sister while my mother was at services with my father.

While I don't remember much of the details of that evening, a few memories remain with me to this very day four decades later. The power went out on that winter evening, and I was terrified in our dark house with my little sister. Together, she and I jumped in our parents' bed and waited for them to get home.

While this story might typically prompt a phone call to Child Protective Services, it does not elicit in me feelings of anger or disappointment. Instead, I am taken by a feeling of compassion. As the father of four children, I can't even imagine what it must have been like for my mother to leave her seven-year-old son in charge of her five-year-old daughter on a cold winter night. What I do know with certainty is that she must have felt tremendous pressure to be present at the service to have left her kids alone that night.

But growing up in the home of a rabbi wasn't all bad. I also remember vicariously experiencing the numerous moments of joy as well. To be a rabbi is to inspire people and help people, and my father was quite excellent at what he did.

Of course, it is easy to reflect on growing up in a clergy house now that I am an adult, and a rabbi. While I was going through it, I did not have the benefit of honest introspection. Instead I was a kid and a teenager, and I saw the world through the prism of a basketball-playing young person. In fact, as I aged, I found myself becoming more distant from the clergy world. As long as my father's job didn't interfere with my life, which it rarely did, I was oblivious to the realities of being a rabbi.

Things changed for me in college—not spiritually, but communally. I worked for two years at a local synagogue as a youth group advisor. I connected with the campus Hillel house, which was the Jewish student association. I took a few Jewish studies classes, and I attended services from time to time as well. Indeed, there was something drawing me to Judaism, but it was not tangible enough for me to understand.

And then, at some point during the second semester of my senior year of college, it occurred to me that I had no plan for the year after college. I had been so focused on getting through college that I had no plan for what would happen once I achieved that goal. *I'll be a rabbi*, I thought. *I can do that.* I remember what it was like for my father. He was a preacher and a social activist. I could do that.

And so, off I went to the Reform Rabbinical School, Hebrew Union College, for my first year in Israel and four subsequent years in Cincinnati, Ohio. During these five years of training, we were taught text and more text—Bible, Midrash, Talmud, and history. My classmates and I were not trained in pastoral counseling or spiritual care; we were trained in our texts. My seminary didn't teach us about how we form a relationship with God or how we best minister to the needs of our congregation; instead it taught us how to be comfortable with the texts of our sacred tradition.

I remember professors of mine remarking that being a pastor was important, but it did not define us as rabbis. What defined us as rabbis was an ability to understand our texts and interpret them for our congregation. After all, how could someone legitimately call him- or herself a rabbi without knowing the words of our tradition?

Though I agree with my professors, ironically, the people I serve don't really care about our ancient texts. The Midrash and Talmud, which were written sixteen hundred years ago, are valuable to our people, but they were written in a different time and express the urges and worries of a different people. Our modern needs have changed much since the days immediately after the destruction of the Second Temple in 70 CE.

But what are those needs? That seems to be the hard part. Depending on the person, the need is likely different. Some people come to the synagogue to pray. They desire to quench a spiritual thirst. Others come to our services because the readings are meaningful or the sermons are inspirational or the music is elevating.

Others come to the synagogue on Sunday morning alone. They drop their kids off for religious school and come back to pick them up two hours later. That is it. Still others find nourishment from the adult education that is offered. It is their brains and not their spirits that are prioritized.

And there is even a group that see the synagogue as the vehicle for making the world a better place. When the prophet Micah reminded us that God wants us to do justice and love mercy (Micah 6:8) or when the prophet Isaiah challenged us by asking if fasts are really what God wants (Isa. 58:6), these were the exhortations of a tradition demanding that we commit ourselves to social justice.

So how can I be all things to all people all at the same time? For me, one answer was not in a textbook but in a realization.

In the book of Genesis, as Abraham leaves Ur of the Chaldees (Gen. 11:31), God tells Abraham to go to the land of Canaan. It is in Canaan that God will make Abraham's name great (Gen. 12:2). It is Canaan that will be an everlasting possession of our people. This is why Jacob and Joseph insisted that when they died, they be brought out of Egypt and buried in Canaan (Gen. 47:29 and 50:25). This was the destination of Moses as he journeyed through the wilderness. He would reclaim that which was lost to us during our years of slavery. Our people have always seen ourselves linked to Canaan and Israel.

King Saul fought the Philistines for it. King David unified our people to make a claim on it. King Solomon enhanced it and built it. In fact, the entirety of 1 and 2 Kings is a rationalization for how and why we lost Israel and went into exile. As the psalmist (likely Jeremiah) puts it best, "By the waters of Babylon, there we sat and wept" (Ps. 137:1 ESV).

Fast forward to the destruction of the second temple, and again we see the pain of our people. They do not lament the loss of a religion. For our ancestors, the reshaping of our religion was welcomed. The cultic sacrificial practices had become outmoded, and a new method for worshipping God was required. But, even as we were happily modernizing our rituals, one thing remained unchanged: a desire to return to Zion, to Israel.

At every worship service, a prayer was added for the return to Zion. Poetry was written to articulate the yearning in our hearts. Consider the Spanish medieval poet Judah Halevi, who wrote, "My heart is in the East, but I am stuck all the way in the West."

In fact, it was at the Sixth Zionist Congress held in 1903 in Basel,

Switzerland, that Theodor Herzl suggested that returning to Israel might be too complicated. Instead, he said, we should settle Uganda in Africa as the new Jewish state. Though the prospect of security for an increasingly vulnerable and consistently harassed people was tempting, the Zionist congress rejected the Uganda plan because Israel had always been our ancestral and spiritual homeland.

After living in Israel for a year in 1992 and having visited her more than thirty times, I feel that I am supremely aware of the importance of Israel to the heart of the Jewish people. The people living in Israel are my family. They worship in different ways, but they are my family. Indeed, 50 percent of the population sees itself as secular and not religious. Still, regardless of how worship styles may vary, the people of Israel are my family.

The State of Israel is the physical representation of the Jewish people. It may be guided by Jewish principles, but its character is one of peoplehood.

As a rabbi, I provide spiritual care for my people by connecting them with *our* people. While it is true that different people present with different types of spiritual care needs, I believe that the spiritual hearts of most people yearn for a sense of connection and purpose. When members of my community see themselves as part of a people with a long history and vibrant heritage, it adds meaning to their spiritual core.

In 1897, at the First Zionist Congress, which was also convened in Basel, Theodor Herzl described his vision for Israel. He remains the "father of modern Zionism" because he had the resources and connections to follow up on his eloquent articulation of a Zionist vision. He was not, however, the only Zionist visionary. And his was not the sole vision. Asher Ginsberg, who changed his name to Ahad Ha'am, also had a vision. And while the distinction between the two might seem small, it was not. For Theodor Herzl, the establishment of the State of Israel meant a *"state of Jews."* For Ahad Ha'am, it meant a *"Jewish state."*

For Theodor Herzl, Israel was the place that a Jew could live in safety and security—not as a second-class citizen or, worse, in a foreign nation. Israel was the representation of the Jews as an ethnic identity.

Ahad Ha'am argued that Israel was a Jewish state in which the rhythms of the Jewish calendar and the rituals of the Jewish people defined the character of the nation. Indeed, Ahad Ha'am was greatly influential, especially in creating a passionate insistence on Israel serving as our destination and not Uganda, as mentioned earlier regarding the Sixth Congress. Still, it was Herzl who ultimately defined the essence of Zionism.

I share this because, as I serve as a spiritual caregiver to the people of my community, I am fully aware of these two principles. For some people, being a Jew is exclusively about being connected to a people. It is not about how we worship, our dietary practices, or the nuances of our rituals. It is simply about belonging to a people and a heritage. These are the Herzls of my community.

For others, being a Jew is about observance less than it is about identity. They are Jews who care about our holidays and our prayers and what our sages say to instruct our lives. These are the Ahad Ha'ams of my community. Interestingly, most people in my community claim to be more akin to Ahad Ha'am but, after some personal exploration, realize they are more connected to Herzl.

Every other year, I lead a trip to Israel for members of my congregation. The participants are families and empty nesters and singles. It is not geared towards any one specific demographic. We usually begin the trip in Jerusalem and travel to the Galilee in the north, Tel Aviv and Haifa to the west, and Masada and the Negev in the south. Starting in Jerusalem can be a very spiritual experience. After all, we spend a great deal of time in the Old City, which brings us to the heart of our ancient faith. The Western Wall is the last and closest remaining element of the Second Temple that was destroyed in 70 CE. There is no question that the first time you place your hands on that wall, you feel something electric. Yes, visiting the Old City of Jerusalem and the Western Wall can be quite an inspiring experience.

And yet, visiting the wall only serves to set up a more profound realization that comes not when a person is praying at the wall or visiting an historically consequential site. Rather, this realization comes when a person is sitting on a towel eating ice cream on the beach of

Ashkelon, buying groceries at a store in Haifa, or filling up their car with gas at a filling station in Tel Aviv. Everyone is Jewish. We are not foreigners in a strange land. This is our land. The lifeguard in Ashkelon is a Jew. The grocery bagger in Haifa is a Jew. The gas station attendant in Tel Aviv is a Jew. When a Jew is in Israel, he or she sees him- or herself as part of a greater Jewish world. And that brings a Jew comfort. Spiritual care is comfort.

The same can be said when hiking through the Judean or Negev desert in the southern part of Israel. I lead people on a hike through the middle of the desert. They are hot, they are tired, and they are usually surprised by how they are challenging themselves and their "comfort zones." Their minds are generally focused on completing this exciting task. But then I stop in the middle of the hike and ask the participants to pause from their walking and close their eyes.

I read to them the story of Elijah hearing the still, small voice in the desert (1 Kings 19:12), and I share that the very hikes we are doing are likely the same ones that the patriarchs Abraham, Isaac, and Jacob walked, in addition to the prophet Elijah.

Or we hike up Nahal Arugot in Ein Gedi, a river oasis in the Judean desert whose source is the winter rain that fell in Jerusalem. As we walk between the tall mountain walls that were carved by the river, I point out the caves high up to the left and right now occupied only by ibex. We pause and read the story of how a young David hid in these caves from King Saul (1 Sam. 24:1–2).

When people experience the modernity of a country in juxtaposition with the biblical history of this very same place, we are comforted by the resiliency, history, and continuity of our people. And that brings a Jew comfort. Spiritual care is comfort.

The second focus I have for providing spiritual care is through textual study. Judaism is a text-based faith. The Bible was the first text but not the last. After the destruction of the Second Temple, our sages compiled an initial corpus of Jewish law that was based upon the Bible, called the Mishnah. The Mishnah served as the focus of intense debate and conversation, which was recorded in a work called the Talmud. The Talmud spoke to the needs of those living at the time but could not foresee circumstances that would emerge over the centuries after its completion. Our tradition has produced volumes of written material addressing modernity vis-á-vis Jewish law.

To study all the texts with members of my congregation would take centuries, not decades. So the textual study within our walls has focused on the original source, the Jewish Bible. Perhaps Bible study is not such a unique pathway to spiritual care. I can imagine many clergy members studying the Bible as a gateway to spirituality. However, my methodology is different.

As a liberal rabbi, I am not insistent on the Bible being the word of God. Indeed, I am a product of the *Wissenschaft des Judentums*, the nineteenth-century German movement of critically studying Jewish texts. I am fully open to the reality of the origin, authorship, and purpose of the Bible. And, more importantly, I am eager to share this discipline of academic biblical criticism to those who study with me. I believe in the documentary hypothesis, which speaks to four distinct authors of the Bible. I believe that much of the Bible was written in stages over a period of two hundred years, taking great shape during the period of Babylonian exile.

One might reasonably think, then, that my teaching undermines my attempt to provide spiritual care. After all, if I question God as being the author of our text and further question God as being the primary actor in the text that the Bible tries to communicate as history, then I am not left with anything spiritually relevant.

Said differently, if God is not the author of the Bible, then why should a person look to the Bible as a source of truth? Or if God's actions in the Bible are not God's actions at all but rather the hopes and wishes of our biblical author, again, why should a person seek out spiritual inspiration from a character in a fictional account?

And yet, still I lead weekly discussions on the text, and the numerous people who engage in them are spiritually uplifted. How? Why? It is because I believe that being honest about the text can lead to even greater spirituality.

In my experience, I have noticed an increased weariness when it comes to speaking about God. So often, a person's theology is more of a Maimonidean reflection of what we believe God to not be. God is not a man, God does not live in a house, God is not Caucasian, God does not speak English. But when it comes to what God is, people are more hesitant to identify these attributes.

The same can be said for the stories of God in the Bible. God is not the being who would advocate for the entire city of Jericho to be destroyed and all its inhabitants killed (Joshua 6). God would not want Abraham to kill his son (Gen. 22) and would not instruct the Israelites to steal the belongings of the Egyptians as they were preparing for the Exodus (Exo. 12:35–36). These depictions of God are unacceptable to the modern reader. So why should I force myself to intellectually rationalize things that are untenable in the first place? The answer, of course, is that I don't.

Still, one might correctly observe that disabusing a person of a flawed (in my opinion) understanding of God as the primary biblical actor does not automatically come with a spiritual replacement. In other words, teaching someone what didn't happen does not presume what did happen.

That is why biblical study comes with a caveat. Studying the Bible is loving the Bible. The words of God or Moses or Isaiah may not specifically provide spiritual care, but the knowledge that the Bible has been our spiritual essence for three thousand years can provide spiritual care. The Jewish family tree goes back one hundred fifty generations. The Bible has been with us for one hundred generations. The vast majority of that family tree took the words of our scriptures as divine, and those generations matter to me. When I help a person see themselves as part of a greater historical timeline, it provides that person with deep spiritual care.

There is another chief practice for spiritual care that I employ—that is through simple one-on-one interactions. People come to me quite often looking for guidance. Sometimes I have it, and sometimes I don't. And yet, generally speaking, the times when I receive the strongest positive feedback come when I have very little guidance to offer.

If a person is struggling with his marriage, the best I can do is reflect on my own marriage and speak without judgment. Using the second-century Talmudic sage Rabbi Akiva as the paradigm for marriage is irrelevant and insulting.

If a person is suffering with illness, offering psalms or prayers as a means toward healing is absurd. The person coming to me didn't want a prayer; he wanted someone to cry with.

When a new and raw mourner looks to me for guidance when the pain of his loss is still very fresh, he is not interested in being told that the loved one is now in a "better place." The better place for everyone is for that person to still be alive and breathing in our home with us.

Spiritual care through counseling is most effective when the spiritual caregiver drops the arrogant need to provide answers and allows uncomfortable ambiguity to carry the day.

I am a rabbi tasked with the unenviable responsibility of providing spiritual care to a group that is widely varied in terms of its needs. Still, despite the confusion, most will agree that spiritual care is supremely important, even though it is increasingly hard to define. My task as a rabbi is to make my way through the complicated landscape.

A Work in Progress

The Rev. Torrence M. Harman

Ring the bells that still can ring
Forget your perfect offering
There's a crack in everything
That's how the light gets in
(from "Anthem" by Leonard Cohen)

My Journey

I t is said that a maze is a place where people lose their way and that a labyrinth is a place where people find their way.

As a child, I remember exploring the English boxwood maze located behind what was then known as Battle Abbey in Richmond, Virginia, the headquarters of the Virginia Historical Society where my grandparents were frequent visitors. The old boxwoods were much taller than I was, but there was a special excitement as I sought and entered the pathway leading in. I don't remember being scared, but my senses seemed a bit sharper, edgy, intently focused on my surroundings and the location of the sun overhead, my bearings seeking intuitive choices. I remember keying into my surroundings and embracing the mystery of the way in, through, and out again.

It would be many years later, with a lot of mileage behind me, that I would discover labyrinths, portable ones spread out on sanctuary floors and stone, dirt, gravel, or grass ones laid out in yards, fields or woods. The labyrinth pattern of entering, releasing, centering, and returning matched the rhythm of transition and discernment times that seemed to come over and over again in my life, often unexpectedly, as I had to let some old ways and outdated dreams die to give birthing room for new ones.

Pictures of pathways (both on land and water) have always had an iconic draw for me—the pathways that turn into bends in the perceived road, pathways that lead toward an unknown beyond, pathways that beckon to other shorelines where sea meets sky. The Celtic notions of "thin places" and "thresholds" stir my spirit. Such horizons have always lured me in special ways, the space between the "now" and the "next" drawing me forward. Like all human beings, I have stood at crossroads, found myself standing in doorways with a choice to go back or to move through and beyond to something new as I am forced to focus on what has been, examine what is happening, and then consider what it might take to open wider the eyes of my heart and mind and step forward onto new landscapes and toward waiting horizons.

I currently serve as an Episcopal priest in the Diocese of Virginia, as a spiritual director, and as adjunct faculty teaching religion courses (Old Testament, New Testament, Religions in America, and World Religions) at Rappahannock Community College in Virginia. The locations where I teach for the college include both on-campus sites populated mostly with millennials trying to find their way in adult life and a nearby state prison housing nine hundred inmates who, for a "time" to be served, find themselves cast out of the mainstream of outside-world life.

My vocational background also includes significant community volunteer work in my twenties and early thirties, primarily focusing on social justice issues and organizational dynamics in not-for-profit and volunteer organizations; law and mediation in my forties and fifties, focusing on divorce, family law, and family mediation; and ultimately at age sixty ordination in the Episcopal Church, serving initially as an assistant rector in a large twenty-five-hundred member midtown urban church and then for the past ten years in small churches in rural areas.

The movement out of law was necessitated by my growing unease with the intense conflict and emotional violence of divorce and other family issues being played out in a combative environment in which I felt I was losing my soul. I had to find a new path in which I was part of processes that built up life rather than tore it apart.

Drawn to smaller parish life during this past decade, I have served "family size" congregations in small communities that operate like extended family systems, with all the positives and negatives that may manifest in such systems. These churches are located in communities with flat demographics and fluctuating dynamics among those who have lived in the area for generations and the more recent retiree "come-heres." There is a still lingering undercurrent of racial tension present in the community systems. In these small rural churches, the rituals embracing birth, baptism, communion, marriage, healing, confession, death, and other transitional life events needing prayer and spiritual care are played out in ways and with the expectation that the priest is needed or may be a part of the process. Small churches are uniquely intimate settings, extremely sensitive to the ebb and flow of the members of the church family. The luminous web of life within a small congregation springs at the lightest touch, and the tremor is felt throughout.

Never in my wildest imagination as a child or teen could I have visualized the vocational paths that emerged for me over time. Born a girl during World War II and growing up in the 1950s in Virginia, what would emerge for me in my time and in my family of origin simply did not anticipate participation in the professions of law and clergy that would become environments in which I would live and move and have my being for half my life.

But a "river runs through it." I am a child of early divorced parents, was partially raised by grandparents (grandfather an Episcopal minister), got married at eighteen, was a mother of three by age twenty-six, became a college graduate finally at age thirty-six, was painfully divorced, got remarried, am now a grandparent of thirteen and a survivor of several major life transitions, and now at age seventy-three, the "river" of my life continues to flow with themes woven into it throughout. Home: Where is it? What is it? Family: What is it? Who is it? Neighborhood/ community: How do we live together in community in ways that enhance all of the life within it? And finally, God, the God of both the religious institutions I attended throughout my life and the wider world where, in my observation, God seemed to roam more freely: Where is God in all of this, and what is our connection with and response to this "Greater-than" that goes by various names dependent on the world view of the speaker?

There is an actual river that informs my image of how life works. I grew up spending summers at my grandparents' cottage on the Rappahannock River, near where it flows into the Chesapeake Bay. When my children came along, they played in its waters on its opposite shore at their paternal grandparents' home right at the mouth of the bay. I returned there permanently when I became a rector of two small historic churches in the area in January 2007.

I have lived one hundred feet from this river for the past decade. The ebb and flow of it, the currents deep and shallow, the energy of it, and the cycle of life it shares with its surroundings inform my view of life. Every evening the sun sets over the horizon where river and shore merge with sky. Every morning the same sun rises, spreading light once again on the fields behind our home where corn, wheat, and soybeans rotate in season—the soil enriched by fallow times and rotating in turn with growing times to assure more abundance. A short distance away is the beautiful in-the-woods paved stone labyrinth located at the 1669 church I last served before I retired as its rector in January 2017. People still stop and mention the Easter sunrise services held in that space each spring as darkness was broken open by the dawn when the light re-emerges on Easter morning. People around here, drawn to retire here, or born here and drawn to remain here appear especially sensitive to the rhythms of nature that seem to mirror the spiritual rhythms of their lives. This may be especially true for many people who live in rural country areas.

Along the Way

In my early fifties, I was introduced to the idea of examining life as a "spiritual journey." This occurred during Education through Ministry (EFM), a four-year course offered through the University of the South at Sewanee. This spiritual practice continued during the time I was exploring a call to ordained ministry and then multiple times in that ordination process. Each time I worked through this exercise, it seemed to shed new light on my journey. The time line and insights that emerged from this spiritual practice surprised me. The revelation that where I met "God" in whatever form I might have considered the "Greater-than" in my life at any given time seemed to happen during the most difficult transitions, the deepest traumas, and the rock-bottom experiences I had along the way. At these times in these places, I found or was found by a Source that was powerfully regenerative. In those times in those places, I seemed to be reconnected with Something or Someone who was intimately present for me and uniquely operating at and as the center and ground of my being.

Ironically, my professional vocations of law, mediation, and priest and my personal life events, which appear to have been continual maze-traveling, labyrinth-exploring, and river-watching, seem to be internally congruent with a life of sitting, being, and working with people at the transitions, the crossroads, and the cross-currents of their lives. As I look back over my life, I believe I was destined for and being prepared to be with folks during those transition times when the way through is disorienting and deconstructive. What Source I had connected with in *my* transition times apparently wanted to use me (whether I was aware of it or not) as a conduit for care for others in *their* transition times.

My license to practice law had identified me and everyone else so licensed as an "attorney and counselor at law." In divorce and family law, it was the counselor aspect that seemed to dominate. My job was to help and facilitate, negotiate and advocate for people going through what for many was a painful and disassembling transition as families were broken apart, with children and possessions allocated. Dreams collapsed, and I sat with folks trying to gather what was left of them and begin to plan how and with what they may piece together a new life.

My work in family law and mediation (as had happened in many circumstances within my family and communities of origin) educated me on a variety of issues that, as I look back, became part of the experience and skill set that would prove so useful in the contexts of later vocational life. These included issues of alcohol and drug abuse, family conflict/ violence and abuse, trauma (both physical and mental), sexuality, aging, intergenerational communication and conflict, estrangement, vocational decision making, financial and economic dis-ease, grief and loss, death and dying, and so on. As a mediator in family matters I tried to help parties bring some order out of their chaos—not only in the arena of divorce and custody but also in the environment of elder law, where controversies about the care of and authority over aging family members and family assets forced the redefinition of intergenerational relationships and yet-to-come continued transitions that would affect family dynamics and even relationships in the generations to come.

Pastoral caregiving was at the heart of my vocational life change as I moved toward and into ministry in faith-based contexts. These contexts included a chaplaincy internship at a continuing care facility; clinical pastoral education in the Virginia Commonwealth University program at the Medical College of Virginia, one of the then seven major trauma centers on the East Coast; and then ultimately in parish settings, as well as spiritual direction with individuals and groups after training through the Washington, DC–based Shalem Institute. While the Hebrew word *Shalom* refers to peace, the Hebrew word *Shalem* refers to health and wholeness. Shalem's spiritual guidance programs train people to be with and guide groups and individuals seeking health and wholeness. What is remarkable about this way of spiritual caregiving is that the apparent caregiver also experiences the transformation of healing and wholeness in the process of being with others.

Spiritual Care

In the September 2016 issue of *The Journal of Pastoral Care and Counseling*, in his editorial "Spiritual Care in Action," Terry R. Bard briefly outlines the emergence of the current societal focus on spiritual care. He comments, "'Spiritual care' now accompanies or replaces 'pastoral care.' Concomitantly, providing this kind of care became enhanced and transformed. Over time, those providing care accommodated to this shift, and it is now robust."[44]

Factors identified as resulting in this shift include "challenges to social norms including cultural and religious shifts in Western world countries" and more people turning "away from more formalized religious traditions and toward more Eastern alternatives in efforts to enhance their own spiritual journeys."[45]

It is interesting to me that the religion classes at the community college where I serve as adjunct faculty include smaller numbers, averaging twelve to twenty for the survey courses in Old Testament and New Testament, while the Religions in America and Religions in the World courses draw significantly more. In summer 2016, the Religions in America course had an initial capacity-filled enrollment of sixty students between its two campuses. Perhaps students are seeking broader perspectives and a more interactive, diverse treatment of religion as they choose a religion elective.

Textbooks now include increased coverage of the growing population of those who label themselves "spiritual but not religious." Those who are unaffiliated with a religious tradition swell the ranks of the "nones" ("none of the above" religious categories) in Pew Institute research on the religious landscape of America. Religious leaders and congregations, whatever their faith tradition, wonder just what it may take to gather these folks into their folds. These trends also challenge spiritual care providers as outdated labels no longer stick and traditional approaches require enhanced and even new processes.

---

[44] Terry R. Bard, "Editorial," *Journal of Pastoral Care & Counseling* (September 2016) 175.

[45] Ibid.

A growing challenge I experience whenever I am with people in what they are experiencing as transition times in life is our vocabulary as we explore what is happening. The secular and sacred vocabularies seem to be shifting, and how they intersect in times of discernment needs a specialized GPS (Global Positioning System) to navigate the ways in, through, and beyond certain life events. I once read a sermon and then quoted the preacher in one of my Sunday homilies when he parsed "GPS" as a God Positioning System. *Clever*, I thought, but I wondered later if it passed the forty-eight-hour shelf life of most sermons. The robustness of spiritual care may be cause for celebration by editors of major journals, but the challenges of such energy, vitality, and potential transformation circulating in our dramatically volatile secular and religious landscapes give pause for care providers who are called to navigate and help develop revised road maps with those who seek guidance in our paradigm-shifting world today, where even the street signs are changing.

In the most recent updated and revised edition of Howard Clinebell's book *Basic Types of Pastoral Care and Counseling*, the author offers an image of what may be becoming increasingly obvious to many: continental plates that undergird our world are shifting and shaking.[46] Of course, the author is using a physical, geographical image as an analogy for what is happening in our communal and spiritual lives in this global village in which we live, move, interact, and have being. The author notes that among the factors causing this are cycles of violence, suffering, and collective evil; the growing complexity of understanding "truth" in any given field; global cybernetic communication networking; scientific research and technology; health-care breakthroughs; increasing globalization; and the mapping of galaxies at the extreme reaches of the universe, confronting humankind with new perspectives and questions about our real place in the universe.[47] The author concludes, "These profound changes challenge many of our aspirations and beliefs,

---

[46] Howard Clinebell, *Basic Types of Pastoral Care & Counseling* (Nashville: Abingdon Press, 2011), 17–18.
[47] Ibid., 18–19.

together with the values, philosophies, and guiding images of the human family. They create enormous pressures on persons, including those who are unaware of the changes. Much of the violence, turmoil, conflict, meaninglessness, value confusion, and spiritual vacuums that increase the need for skilled caregiving is rooted in this radical shaking of society's foundational beliefs, values, and structures."[48]

Perspectives and Reflections

I have been profoundly impacted by my grounding in Judeo-Christian thought and action. However, my life has not been static. Whatever homeostasis (the tendency of the body to seek and maintain a condition of balance and equilibrium within its internal environment, even when faced with external changes) may have characterized my life at any given time has been challenged by the operation of both internal and external forces.

In my early fifties after the death of my mother, during a time of increasing dissatisfaction with what I was doing vocationally and challenges prompting me to come out of what seemed to be spiritual hibernation, I entered counseling with a remarkable woman. I remember her as a wise guide as I was traveling the fault lines of a personal midlife continental-plate shifting. Before our last session, she prescribed homework for me. I was to consider what I might choose to have on my gravestone when I died. I needed to come up with something in the two-week interval before our next session. What a question! It was as if I were being asked to review the book of my life, chapter by chapter; reflect; and then come up with a title for volume two.

Finally, the night before I was to see the counselor again, an image appeared to me. One of my daughters was a fine arts dance major at Virginia Commonwealth University in Richmond. I attended all of the students' dance recitals but was most drawn to and intrigued by the impromptu recitals—not finished products, but performances offered

---

[48] Ibid., 19.

as works in progress. The next morning, I shared with my counselor the inscription: "A Work in Progress by the Grace of God."

Whatever I may offer as perspectives and reflections on spiritual care in this essay are continually evolving. I have been stretched and molded by every pastoral and spiritual contact that the Divine has placed in my path. My boundaries, which I hope are basically healthy, have become more permeable as I have been exposed to other faith traditions and deeper, broader spiritual currents than I may have originally felt possible in the theology of my traditional Christian upbringing. I am a lifelong learner, and I believe God has a few more miles for me to go before I am called to rest into what life beyond has in the Divine mind and heart for me. So, knowing that the observations and reflections I have shared so far and the ones that follow are incomplete, I offer them in the spirit of our continual evolution as servants of a living God.

Spirit

What is contemplated as the "spirit" in spiritual care? Two possibilities that I suggest offer a both/and approach. The Spirit of God is referenced throughout the Hebrew scriptures and the Christian New Testament. The Spirit of God is portrayed variously as the force bringing order out of chaos at creation; as the animating, creating, and sustaining energy of God; as the allocating entity that apportions the God-given gifts of the Spirit; and as the generative force of God.

I remember being with Julia, one of the elder members of one of the country churches I served (Trinity Church, known as the Little Church with a Big Heart in Lancaster County, Virginia). She was declining, moving into that time that operates as a bridge between the now and the hereafter. She reminisced about some of her favorite times at Trinity, particularly as a former teacher of what comprised a one-room Sunday school there. "I loved teaching the children about the Holy Spirit," she began. "On a windy Sunday, I would bring plastic bags that I collected at home and give one to each of the children and then send them out into the churchyard to catch the wind. Filled and then caught by the wind around them, the bags became alive, dancing and sailing around above their heads. 'You know,' I would tell the children, 'the Holy Spirit is like the wind. You can't see it, but you know it's there when it fills something and makes it move.'" I relayed this story to some of the parishioners who I thought may have been children in her class. They just smiled. And, remembering Julia's story, I watched them as I saw the Spirit move in their lives over time.

The other possibility in this "both/and" view is the spirit of the individuals who seek the care of the Spirit for the care of their individual spirits. Again, *spirit* here may be seen as an animating generative force within us—experiencing vitality/depression, health/disease, wholesomeness/woundedness, active or passive, awake or asleep within us at various times and during various events in our lives.

Are not those called into the ministry of spiritual caregiving drawn into a divine dance as our spirit and the other's spirit are joined by the Holy Spirit, filling, moving, and guiding us toward the promise of wholeness and a new way of living and being.

Context/Worldview

If "location, location, location" is the mantra for discernment of the value and viability of a piece of property in a real estate market, then "context, context, context" is a good mantra to remember in spiritual care. Consideration of the contexts in which a person has been or currently is located as they seek spiritual care is important. Consideration of our own contexts as we are with them is important. Context forms and informs the interpretive vocabulary we use as we explore and discern the meaning of what is happening in people's lives and their responses to it.

Context shapes an individual's worldview. Our worldview shapes the lenses through which we view life and what is happening in it to us. These contexts include our gender; race; age; ethnicity; culture; family of origin; places where we have lived; friendships; personal, local, national, and worldwide events that have impacted us; and even our parents, religious orientation and background, education, socioeconomic status, life experiences, and so on. Spiritual care does not require a multipage interview component. However, an awareness of the elements that have shaped our lenses and the lenses of those with whom we meet is useful as the Spirit who, of course, knows all guides us and uses us to help others.

Storytelling

Storytelling and story-listening play a major role in spiritual care. When in need of care, people have a deep desire to share what has happened to them, often offered in the form of a story. Like ancient peoples trying to understand how things came into being and why things are the way they are, we become storytellers as we try to make meaning of what we experience and seek purpose for ongoing existence given what is happening around us. We tell stories to support what appear to be our conclusions about how life is lived and why things are the way they are to us. We tell stories to draw one another into our story line to understand who we are and why we act the way we do, hoping that our listeners will better understand us and connect with us as they resonate with our stories. We have communal stories that operate to gather and bind people together in shared understandings and expectations. There are archetypal stories that transcend time and place and operate within the deepest levels of our human "being."

Clergy and lay pastoral caregivers know that people who experience loss so often want to tell, over and over again, the story of the loss and the events surrounding it. It is as if they are trying to get a handle on what has happened, to make sense of facts and feelings that are real but terribly painful, to explore deeply what has happened, and to travel through the question "Why?"

The storyteller may offer or dwell on stories that are found elsewhere but operate as symbolic and relevant for the storyteller's situation. Care providers may guide someone in need of spiritual care to reflect on a story in their faith tradition or a story from their culture that may stir recognition and new insight on a situation. Whether a caregiver shares one of his or her own stories requires careful assessment, self-awareness, other-awareness, and realistic consideration of motive and intent in deciding to share or not.

Listening

Storytelling in spiritual and pastoral care situations raises consideration of the art and science of "listening." Effective active listening requires engagement. It requires a willingness to enter into the world of the speaker, embracing what is being said and how it is being offered, combined with a healthy and loving detachment that is needed for good perspective.

Experts agree that communication is composed of verbal and nonverbal elements. Communication includes what is said (the words), how it is said (voice, tone, inflection, etc.), and nonverbal body language, which may give off messages that are congruent, noncongruent or in addition to or in negation of what is being verbalized. Good listening takes practice— it's like juggling several balls in the air at the same time. It requires application of eyes, ears, head, heart, gut, and that place where intuition moves within us, offering to take part in the action.

As a pastor, it has always been important to me to visit parishioners who have recently been through traumatic times (accident, illness, surgery, death of a loved one, experiencing chronic conditions that isolate them, in distress over events happening to others in their family systems, etc.). I tell them, "I really want to be with you in person and see how you are doing with my own two eyes." Yet, in the practice of spiritual direction, while my preference is always for us to meet in person, some of our most powerful times have been when the meeting has had to be conducted by phone for reasons such as travel or other distance-causing situations. I still, as usual, take time out before the long-distance meeting to hold the person on my heart, even visualizing them and then tapping into the Source that I trust desires to connect all things. I move my chair in front of an almost floor-to-ceiling window to face the river flowing by a hundred yards away from me. I key into the natural flow I both see and sense and then make the call to the one waiting to talk with me. We both remind ourselves of the Third Party with us as we offer a simple prayer, opening to the presence of the Spirit on the line with us.

Presence

Spiritual care is all about presence—our being present with those seeking spiritual care in a way that they know we are there for them, focused on them and their situation, that they experience our orientation toward them as their having immense value in the eyes of God, that our way with them honors their worth and respects their dignity, and that we are there for them, being used by God as a conduit for God's compassion and healing love.

Spiritual care is all about *the* Presence—about connecting with the energy of God manifested by God's Spirit that is always present to us and those God places in our path. It is the Spirit always operating to bring about healing and wholeness. Spiritual caregiving calls the giver and receiver to open to the presence of the Spirit and cooperate with its restorative work. Whenever in doubt in a care context, pause, seek the direction of the Spirit, listen to the divine "voice" within, and then, in faith, proceed.

Self-Awareness/Self-Care

The need to be self-aware in spiritual caregiving situations is obvious. Yet how often are we easily hijacked into trying to fix someone else, to push solutions on them, to interject ourselves into their "stuff," and just generally try to control both process and outcomes? The Source of all healing and caregiving is greater than we are and is always present for us and in our interactions with others (whether we remember this or not). This ever-present Source desires to be the director and guide of outcomes that lead to health, wholeness, and the greater good for those involved.

One of the aha moments in my life happened some time ago in a large metropolitan bookstore. While looking in a section for people needing to find quick, inexpensive Christmas presents, I came across a little book of quotes about God. I began to thumb through it quickly, very much at that moment in need of the gift of enlightenment in my busy life as a "lawyer in recovery" headed for seminary and struggling with whether to enter the intensive path toward ordination. But then I stopped at a quote that caught my attention and proffered a truth approximately worded, "God doesn't expect you to produce results. That's God's job. God just wants you to be faithful." It was as if an immense load was lifted off me. What a relief for someone who was raised with the hope and expectation that I would do "right," do well, perform as perfectly as possible, and always succeed (whatever that meant). And, yes, I was to leave the world a little better place when I died. (Thank you, Grandmother, for that one, though I know you meant well!) My earlier chosen professions of excelling at whatever I did, mothering, and then law fed my "control" tendencies and nurtured an ego driven toward fixing things and meeting others' expectations of excellence. I have remembered this God quote so many times as I found myself slipping back into unhealthy patterns of thinking.

This, of course, brings up the issue of self-care. Essential to being a healthy care provider is to take care of the provider, yourself. Such ways of care may include being part of a mutual ministry support group; selecting and meeting with a trusted spiritual director or guide; seeking professional counseling as may be needed; taking time out for group or personal retreats; intentionally setting apart quiet times and quiet days; and embracing practices that are restorative and connect us with Source and Spirit such as meditation, mindfulness, contemplative prayer, time in nature, yoga, study and reflection on Scripture, and so on. In our busy lives, we need to take intentional times to go to the well; to nurture the relationships among our bodies, minds, hearts, and souls; and to let ourselves be nourished and restored.

There is a story about a South American tribe and a visitor among them studying the tribe's way of life. From time to time, members of the tribe would gather and then take off, traveling at a fast pace for days at a time (perhaps in search of game, better hunting grounds, or a new location for the tribe). After so many days, they would simply stop, set up camp, and stay where they were, pausing before continuing their journey. The visitor who had joined them on their march this time asked the leader of the tribe, "Why are we stopping?" The leader replied, "We are waiting for our souls to catch up with us."

This is wisdom for those called to the ministry of spiritual care.

Simple Things, Simple Ways

In the movie *The Sound of Music,* the nanny, played by Julie Andrews, teaches the children a song, "A Few of My Favorite Things." Just thinking about "whiskers on kittens" and "warm woolen mittens" brings delight to the children as war clouds hover on their horizon.

My spiritual director gave me a small stone that she had brought back from the holy island of Iona. It is a talisman to touch in moments of reflection.

Recently, I used a few multicolored, polished stones I had bought from an old man at a local farmers' market. I scattered them around a candle on a small table in the center of a circle gathering for an Advent evening program. At the end of the evening, each person selected a stone that "spoke" to him or her, one that called "take me home with you"—to be a reminder of light shared on a dark winter's night.

Women gather at a local church, knitting shawls that later find their way to places as close as the continuing-care facility a couple of miles down the road or to someone in a faraway state. One found its way to me as a thank-you gift for leading a weekend retreat for the church. Several months later it served as a warm throw for my legs as I spent many hours on a sofa at home recovering from hip surgery. Into every prayer shawl or lap robe the women weave their prayers for a yet-unknown recipient. The finished shawls, spread around the sanctuary altar and blessed again by the celebrant at a Sunday communion service, are then ready to be sent out as emissaries of comfort and healing.

An altar-guild member rearranges flowers that graced the sanctuary that morning. She then delivers them to a person who just lost someone dear to them, who is recovering from surgery, or who for some unknown reason just sprang to mind as needing something beautiful in his or her life that Sunday afternoon.

At a church in Richmond, a prayer-and-study group crafts origami cranes as the members of the group sit together. The tiny cranes then rest in a woven basket on a table located along a well-traveled pathway through the parish house. A sign offers "Take One," with the explanation that cranes symbolize hope and healing. Two rest on the dashboard of my car. (I am sticking to the story that I made two trips through the parish hall on different days.) The little paper cranes remind me from time to time of someone, including myself, who may need a spiritual "lift" and some hope and healing in their lives, and I offer up a simple prayer.

Someone simply comes to mind or is laid on your heart, and rather than offering a formal prayer, you simply envision a soft, warm light surrounding them, and a sense of peace seems to flow from that moment.

During a golf game, a friend shares with you a situation he is going through, something that is deeply concerning to him and may have a negative impact on his family. You lean into his story, encourage his considering possible ways through this troubled time, and the two of you make plans for lunch next week. "I'm here for you" is the message the friend receives from your attention.

In a time in the service known as Prayers of the People, the congregation names those on their prayer lists. I remember one of the nursing-home-bound women, a member of one of the churches I served. She was on our prayer list Sunday after Sunday. During one of our visits, she told me that she would pause for a time each Sunday morning from about 10:00 to 10:05 a.m. and feel the voices praying for her. The next Sunday I checked my watch when the prayer list names were read. It was a few minutes after 10:00 a.m.

The phone rings, and it's someone calling "out of the blue." There's something in the caller's voice that sounds a need to talk, just talk, and something tells you, "Listen—just listen."

Our Sacred Journey

We don't have to be trained professionals to be a part of the continuum of spiritual caregiving that is needed in this world. We don't need to be formal or fancy. We don't need to prepare artfully formulated prayers or organize large groups of helpers who may become more interested in maintaining the organization and vetting participants than simply serving as conduits of grace. We don't need to absolutely control what, how, and when care is to be given and received. We don't need to prepare to-do lists for the ones seeking care—lists of books to read, exercises to do, places to go, other professionals to consult—although from time to time occasional suggestions among these possibilities are appropriate as guided by the Spirit.

The poet Mary Oliver offers the following poem entitled "Praying."
It doesn't have to be
the blue iris, it could be
weeds in a vacant lot, or a few
small stones; just
pay attention, then patch

a few words together and don't try
to make them elaborate, this isn't
a contest but the doorway

into thanks, and a silence in which
another voice may speak.[49]

God uses us all, in all our ways, whether known or unknown to us. God uses both the complex and the simple. Sometimes it seems though the simple is the most useful for God's purposes; it allows space for the Spirit to move around with what we have to offer. Whatever we bring to the spiritual-care relationship is an imperfect offering, but God consecrates it. And our journey, in God's hands, becomes sacred.

The sacred journey is not easy. The road we travel has places where

---

[49] Mary Oliver, "Praying," *Thirst* (Boston: Beacon Press, 2007), 37.

we are knocked to our knees and cracked wide open. But then, after all, that's how the light gets in. Then God gathers up the pieces of us and shapes us again into useful vessels, serving us up to be a healing balm and to incarnate light on the way to healing and wholeness. And somewhere a holy bell rings in celebration.

Most of the time, all we really need is an open heart, an open mind, a listening orientation, a will willing to "let go and let God," a desire to be connected to and guided by the Spirit of the Source of all life, and the courage to let that happen to us. It sounds complicated, but at the heart of spiritual care is a beautiful and profound simplicity. We are to simply be open to being used by God as a conduit of divine love that creates, redeems, and sustains—a restorative love that promises "I make all things new again."

By God's amazing grace, may we be so!

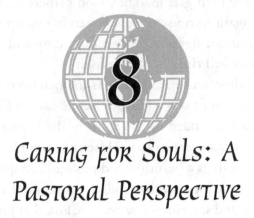

Caring for Souls: A
Pastoral Perspective

Rev. C. Brandon Brewer

For many people, the word *hospice* has a specific connotation: a set of words and images that are undergirded by confusion, fear, and avoidance. Particularly in the African American community, the word *hospice* is synonymous with death—the word no one wants to hear. Language is important; *death* can be too harsh. Therefore, we embrace terms such as *home-going, transition,* and *leaving this earthly vessel for a heavenly one,* to name a few. This is a way in which we can acknowledge the present circumstances while clinging to the hope that is produced by our expressions of faith.

Oftentimes, when I encounter people who learn that I have spent the last five years of my ministry in hospice chaplaincy, the responses range from a complete change of subject and avoidance to nervous smiles and humor. On occasion, I get to witness the blank stare of one deciding if they want to continue having a conversation with me at all. I can recall numerous times being met with comments such as "That must be really difficult" and "I don't know how you do it! I could never work in hospice!" Of course, there are more interesting responses such as, "I bet people in hospice see you as the Angel of Death when you walk in!" I can recall numerous occasions when I was sitting in a worship service at a mostly African American church and hearing the prayer requests for Sister or Brother so-and-so who has been placed on hospice care, and a collective gasp takes over the entire building accompanied by several loud exclamations of "Jesus!" "Have mercy!" "O, Savior!" and "Merciful Father!"

While I have grown accustomed to these types of responses among numerous others, I can easily admit that, years ago, I shared similar thoughts and feelings about hospice care in general, let alone ministry coupled with hospice care. Ministry in end-of-life care is delicate, sensitive, and yet beautiful and rewarding. Oftentimes, people miss or overlook the fact that hospice care is about life: living the best life one can, even when faced with life-threatening illness; providing comfort; finding meaning; embracing hope; having support when facing challenges; and the opportunity for one to dictate his or her own personal growth.

Spirituality is a vital component in the lives of many African Americans, particularly as it relates to decision-making and care options. Certainly, there is no one-size-fits-all or one generalized rulebook that dictates how each person or family is to respond when faced with the challenges of life, but I will say that over the last several years in hospice ministry, I have seen many common themes, approaches, coping mechanisms, and experiences when working with African American families that compel me to tell the stories of how *some* African American families approach difficult times when a family member or loved one is faced with a terminal illness and impending transition from life as we know it to that of the eternal. Within this essay, I include my own story of struggle that bears witness to my own experiences of transition, loss, and growth.

Stories are powerful. Stories shape us and help us grow. They provide opportunities for us to share our experiences; to connect with our thoughts, feelings, and emotions; and to connect with the lives of others. Stories impact us at all ages and stages of life and throughout the human experience with a rich legacy of storytelling that many of us have found encouraging, leading to a greater knowledge of self and perhaps a sense of peace and hope to sustain us on our own journeys. Utilizing this understanding of the deep impact that stories have on the self and others, I would like to share two stories that have shaped me in life and ministry. Within these stories, I include some thoughts and insights that may offer inspiration and hope to others. The first story comes from my ministry experiences as hospice chaplain. The second story is my own—a chronicle of my first personal encounter with hospice care and how it shaped me and my ministry.

One Last Night

One evening when I was working late on a unit at the local hospital, I sat at a big round table in the common waiting area of the unit near the elevators. Mindlessly, I was working on my laptop with paperwork spread all around the table. Occasionally, I would look up and watch the groups of people getting on and off the elevators, wondering who they were there to see and studying their facial expressions to gain clues and insights into what their experiences might be. At one point, a gentleman stepped off the elevator with two other people, one male and one female. At first glance, I didn't pay too much attention to this group of people; however, I remembered this one particular gentleman simply because I had seen him a few moments prior to that, when he first got onto the elevator alone. I noted that he had gone to the café to get food and must have met some arriving family members along the way. Upon his return, he had a basket of fries and a personal-sized pizza. The three of them sat on the couches in the common area near the table where I had created my own personal workstation. The woman (later identified as his sister-in-law) began verbally listing all the reasons that the first gentleman should not be having fries right then. I looked up, glanced at the three of them with a smile, and then returned to what I was working on.

Suddenly, I heard a voice, "Look at this young man! He must be very busy and important around here. He's got all his paperwork spread all over the table. You know, we couldn't sit over there if we wanted to. I wonder if he realizes that he's taking up the whole table. Young man, do you realize you are taking up the whole table?" When I looked up, the gentleman was pointing at me and laughing at his previous comments. I was terribly embarrassed, plus his comment startled me. Frantically, I responded with, "Oh, my goodness, I am so sorry! I didn't realize I was taking up the entire table. I'll make space for you so you can eat. I apologize!"

He sprung up from the couch and said, "I am just joking with you, young man. It's all right, really. I wasn't planning on sitting at the table. Leave your papers there, it's fine." This provided me with instant relief; however, I still felt very ashamed of the fact that I hadn't even considered that someone else may want to sit at the table. We continued our conversation.

Initially, we exchanged names and general pleasantries. As the conversation evolved, we discovered that we had many similar experiences; he was also clergy and the pastor of a small congregation in an adjacent county. The two people with him departed, but he remained in the common area with me. He then said something that captured my attention: "You know, I saw you earlier today. I know it was you because I remembered your shoes. I knew from your shoes that you were in ministry. I was sitting at this very table, and I was writing a letter to my wife to be included in her funeral program. I looked up and you were standing there waiting for the elevator and talking to another guy who was with you. As soon as I finished my letter, I went back to her room, and they told me that her breathing changed. It was as if she knew." I was struck by the fact that this pastor, whom I had watched enter and exit the elevator, had sat at this same table a few hours earlier writing a letter to say goodbye to his wife. Then there was the matter about my shoes. I'm a big fan of square-toed shoes; admittedly, they are unique, but what would cause him to focus on my shoes while preparing to say goodbye to his life partner of over forty years? *Perspective. Reflection. Pause.* Sometimes when we are in a season of anticipatory grief, we see glimpses of life around us that help us latch on to hope, that provide a welcomed distraction and allow us to explore common and sacred moments in our own lives. We create narratives; we create stories; and more importantly, we become a part of the stories of others.

This pastor and I spoke for well over an hour. While I sat talking with him, I wondered to myself, *Why hasn't he gone back into his wife's room* yet? but I dared not ask. I decided to allow the dialogue to run its natural course. "So, tell me, what drew you to hospice?" he asked. I shared with him how difficult it is to put into words; truly, there is something very sacred about hospice ministry. Suffice it to say that I shared with him how amazing it is to journey with people and their families when a person is nearing the end of life. It feeds me, it fuels my passion for people and ministry in a variety of forms, and it is truly a blessing to be invited to take part in the beauty and mystery of one's end-of-life journey. I also shared the importance of simply being present with people when they experience major life changes and transitions. It was refreshing to have him respond in an affirmative manner. He expressed genuine appreciation for people who feel called to serve in hospice ministry.

He then put things into perspective for me by saying, "I understand the importance of being present. This is why I want to spend *one last night* with my wife, just the two of us—one last time." From his perspective, he wanted to be "selfish" and have her all to himself, but as a pastor, father, and friend to many, he didn't want to take the opportunity for them to say goodbye away. After another forty-five minutes of discussion, he decided to send everyone in his wife's room home. He wanted his time alone with his wife, and he was going to have it.

As we wrapped up our discussion, I thanked him for taking the time to share and talk about his experiences. He responded by telling me that he knew I would be a good person to talk with and shared that the reason he made a big scene about my taking up all the space at the round table was because he was trying to find a lighthearted way of engaging me in conversation. He needed a break from being the pastor, husband, caregiver, father, and decision-maker, among the other roles he was juggling while facing the thought of losing his wife. He needed an opportunity to be human and to talk. Little did I know how significant the impact he would have on my life and my ministry would be!

As he was walking away, he said to me, "You have been here all evening and have not eaten anything. Would you like some of my pizza?"

I quickly responded with, "No, thank you! You are very kind to offer, but I won't be here very much longer."

His last words to me as he turned and looked back were, "Okay, but just remember, it was Jesus who offered it to you!" Then he smiled and walked away. His words still strike me today. It wasn't that he was claiming to be Jesus himself, but rather, it spoke to the fact that we both *represented* care, concern, and the love of Jesus to one another and that we were sojourners on this journey of life and loss together. In caring for the soul of another, my soul is filled and enriched! Encounters such as this one highlight the power and vitality of hospice-care ministry.

From My Own Eyes

When asked by the pastor in my previous reflection about what drew me into hospice care, I went back over a decade to my first hospice encounter with one of my grandmother's sisters. The encounter from which this story takes its shape took place in early 2005 when I was in seminary. At the time, I was taking a course called Pastoral Care to Those Facing Loss and Grief. At that stage in my journey, I took the class out of curiosity as I was not comfortable with death, dying, grief, and all related topics. This class stretched me and forced me to step out of my comfort zone.

When I was faced with the challenges of loss and grief within my own family, the material and discussions from my class became real. In part, everything I learned went out the window, but on the other hand, I needed something to help me process my experiences as I began living out this narrative of grief. Then it struck me: what would happen if I started writing a grief journal to keep a chronicle of my thoughts, feelings, and experiences that I could look back on as I work my way through the grieving process? I had thoughts like, *How do I do this? What would it look like? What would I do with it exactly?* I decided to jump in and write.

My journey with hospice began on April 4, 2005. A few of my cousins and I set out for our weeklong Spring Break from Atlanta to Louisiana to be with family. We knew that our great-aunt, "Auntie," had been sick and that two weeks prior, she had been diagnosed with pancreatic cancer and had spent the last week in the hospital. We prepared ourselves for the nearly twelve-hour drive. Secretly, I had a ball of dread, tightly bound and continually growing in the pit of my stomach. I tried to ignore it with the help of music, laughter, and conversation—anything I could find to relieve the mounting fear and anxiety that was internally consuming me.

Things went along just fine across the Alabama state line, through Birmingham, to Tuscaloosa, across the Mississippi state line, and to Meridian. Four and a half hours into our trip, we stopped in Meridian to get lunch. A call came from my mother: "Brandon, Auntie just had an episode this morning, and they thought we were losing her. Call your grandmother and see what's going on." I thought, *Oh, boy! I am not ready for this.* I called my grandmother as we hurried to get back on the road. I didn't like the way she sounded; she seemed a little shaken, which was unusual to me. This signaled a sense of urgency, and I was gripped with fear. For the next four and a half hours of our journey, all I could think about were all the different scenarios lingering on my mind, with each one accompanied by a new wave of fear. But what was I so afraid of?

Monday, April 4

We reached the hospital between five and six o'clock that evening. Many of our family members were already gathered in Auntie's room. We were all exhausted, nervous, quiet, and fearful. I remember vividly my heart being gripped with fear. I did not know how to feel or what to think. Once we got to the hospital, we went to the third floor to see Auntie. It was my moment of truth—the day of reckoning. Whatever fear I felt before we arrived would be met with the reality of what we would find in that hospital room. *Am I ready? Can I just stand in the hall and not go in? What am I supposed to do? Will she be alive still? Will she look scary? Will she have already passed?* These were all the thoughts I had as we hurried to the room. Once we arrived, I had no choice—I had to go in.

Just as we entered her room, Auntie was settling into a very deep sleep; her breathing appeared very labored, as if she would go at any moment. I thought she looked like she was on death's doorstep. Fear was my dinner. My fears were my thoughts. *Fear, fear, fear.* I was afraid. I was afraid that she would die right then and there. She looked so frail. She had lost a lot of weight. She didn't look like herself. I was heartbroken and crestfallen; I tried for several minutes to avoid looking at her altogether. I could feel the collective emotional energy mounting among the family. I thought to myself that it would only be a matter of time before the floodgates opened and we would all be inconsolable.

"Well, the doctor said we can take her home with hospice care," my grandmother said in an even yet resigned tone. The chatter started, and the questions came fast and furious. "Hospice?" "Wait, what? Does it mean *this is it*?" "Is her life over?" "What is hospice?" "What does it all mean?" "Can someone explain to me what's happening?" Then I allowed myself to face it. I looked at Auntie and studied her face. Her hair was very long, though tightly wound into two bun swirls on the top of her head. I was disturbed by the way she slept so rigidly. Just as I began to grasp some of the reality of this situation, a family member said, "Wait, everyone. Let's gather around Auntie. We need to pray as a family. Brandon, you are going to pray for us." *What!* I thought. *No, really, you've got to be kidding. I can't do this; I don't have it in me. I don't even fully understand what's happening yet.* The family gathered around the bed and held hands. They were all waiting on me to start praying. I took a deep breath, closed my eyes, and began to pray. I don't remember what I said in the prayer, but I do remember how people responded to the prayer. Somehow there was hope in the room, a little more peace, greater strength, and the presence of God.

I began seeing my class on grief and loss unfold before my eyes. At one point during class, we passed around a hospice brochure for everyone to read. As I was gathered with my family in Auntie's hospital room, I noticed all the signs from that brochure right in front of my face—medication to keep the patient comfortable, weight loss, lethargy—all the signs were there. I knew then that Auntie would not be with us forever, and it was more apparent than ever before. She slept through the night, and my grandmother and I went back to Auntie's house. My grandmother and I talked, watched television, and went to bed. I was tired. The fear of anticipatory grief wrestled with me all day and all night long.

Tuesday, April 5: Guilt

My grandmother and I woke up, made coffee, and ate a little breakfast. This began *the hard part*. We had to make changes around Auntie's house. The "hospice people" were coming to set everything up, so we had to be ready. But who were these people? What were they going to do?

Later that morning, we went to the hospital. Auntie was awake. *Thank you, Jesus!* I thought. The previous day had me thinking she was gone for sure. But she was up, alert, and ready to talk. She commented on many things; she noticed that I had lost some weight, and we talked about the news and "normal" topics. It was just like old times when I would go and spend time with her as a teenager! Laughter and joy made a guest appearance that day. Auntie told me how much she loved me and how wonderful it was for her to see me. She made me feel good. She affirmed me. She made me feel special.

As I reflected on all of this special attention, I began to feel guilt. I felt guilty because she was in bed, struggling with pancreatic cancer while I had my youth on my side. I could just get up and go on with my life as usual, but she no longer had that luxury. I fought a noble fight with guilt. I couldn't allow it to overtake me; it was not my fault! Within myself I started thinking, *Are you kidding me? This woman has been in church for many, many, years … dedicated herself to church, Sunday school, mission, you name it! This just means that we must pray harder and have an unwavering faith. Surely things will get better. Auntie is going to be just fine.*

That night, my grandmother and other family members spent the night at the hospital. I was left alone at Auntie's house for the night, and I heard every sound that could be heard. To top it all off, there was a terrible thunderstorm with loud thunder and frequent flashes of lightning. As one may imagine, I was feeling a bit nervous, to say the least, and of course at a time like this, I was fully relying on my faith to get me through the night. I slept on the couch in the living room with the television on.

Wednesday, April 6: Hospice

Auntie's sons arrived. They helped get things set up just before the hospice team arrived with a hospital bed and oxygen, among other things. *Okay, fine. Here we go.* The hospital sent Auntie home; we got her settled in the house and tucked nicely into the bed with her oxygen flowing.

A few visitors came, and Auntie was so excited. We made her as comfortable as possible. Then I noticed something: although Auntie was awake and alert, she did not realize that she was in her own house. For long periods of time, she would stare at the ceiling or fix her gaze on a ceramic angel atop her dresser. I suggested to my grandmother that we put a radio in Auntie's room to keep her stimulated. Auntie always had the radio playing in the back room, set on the twenty-four-hour gospel music station. This seemed to help a great deal! She would nod her head, listen to the music, and listen to the preachers. She even said "Amen!" when she could. With all of this, she still seemed to be getting weaker, and she started staring more and more.

Soon, calls from the hospice team members started coming. Throughout the remainder of the week, hospice team members came and went. I tried my best to disengage. I didn't want to be bothered; I didn't want them there. Wasn't hospice a way of admitting defeat? Isn't it considered giving up? As I listened to each of them speak, I noticed that they spoke about hospice care in a way that was different than what I expected. They spoke about hospice in a way that gave us space to be, space to live in our new reality, and space to know that they would be there when we needed them to be. They didn't impose their presence and they didn't promise any miracles, but they supported us throughout the process.

Thursday, April 7: Anger

I was mad. There was no good or gentle way to state it. I was filled with anger. I was angry that I had to see Auntie that way. I was angry at pancreatic cancer. I was angry that I had to deal with ups and downs, broken sleep, fear, and anticipatory grief all at once. It was too much! I had a lot of questions for God.

My grandmother needed a break and hadn't been able to do any shopping, so I stayed at home with Auntie. She was lonely, and it was quiet in the house. I heard Auntie calling out for my grandmother, so I jumped up from the couch and ran to her room. I went and sat at her bedside. She was so happy to see my face! She smiled, and I grabbed her hand, sat with her, and talked to her. After she calmed down and knew that I would be in the house with her, she felt comfortable enough to rest and attempt to sleep. She kept telling me how much my being there meant to her. She said, "You just don't know, but your being here makes me feel so good!" When I left her room, I began to weep. I knew she was declining, I knew this disease was causing her increasing pain, and I knew that soon we would have to choose to keep her comfortable, which meant she may have fewer times when she would be able to engage and converse with us. This was a harsh reality and a wake-up call. In the middle of the night, around four o'clock, I heard her calling out. I immediately sprang out of bed, and my grandmother and I both rushed to her bedside. I was thinking, *Is this it? Is she going? Are we saying goodbye?* No, Auntie was wide awake. She wanted a glass of water. We gave her water and then sat in her room with her until the sun came up.

Friday, April 8: Surrender

This was the day before we were heading back to Atlanta. Auntie looked bad. She was still awake and alert, but the pain was becoming almost unbearable for her. She would grasp her stomach and tell us of more pain. I knew this was not good. She wanted to rest, but friends, neighbors, and church members came by. My grandmother had to start pureeing all of Auntie's food in the blender to make it easier for her to eat because she could no longer chew or swallow solid foods. Exhaustion and fatigue began to settle in. I was tired. There were too many intense emotions to deal with. I was tired, and I knew that Auntie was not going to be around forever. I just didn't know when she was going to go.

Saturday, April 9: Exploration and Acceptance

The time came for my cousins and me to head back to Atlanta. Everyone smothered Auntie with love, hugs, and kisses. When I went to give her a hug, I held her hand for a few minutes, kissed her on her forehead and cheek, and said, "Auntie, I'm about to head back to Atlanta." She replied, "Oh, baby! You're going home too?" It was difficult to leave—very difficult. We packed up the car and left for Atlanta. We spent long periods in silence on the trip back, each one of us trying to find a mental life raft with which to navigate the waters of the thoughts swimming in our heads. On occasion, we would throw out a thought or memory from the week that led to a cascade of repetitious verbal reflections.

Sunday, April 10: Bargaining

I just wanted to bargain—*let's make a deal*, if you will. Phone calls with family members yielded reports that Auntie had stopped talking, eating, and drinking. She would only stare off into space with a fixed gaze. One family member said, "She's got one foot here and one foot in eternity."

The next few days were difficult ones. I went from bargaining to anger and back and forth several times. I was distracted. Surely a miracle was still possible. I just knew that things could turn around. All we needed was a little more prayer.

Tuesday, April 19: Change

This day felt different. I felt lighter than I had in a long time. I was busy; I had fun. It was the first time I had laughed and joked in weeks! I spent time with friends. I felt better until …

Tuesday, April 19, 2005, at 10:00 p.m.: Death

I had such a great day, but it seemed that I had spoken too soon. Auntie died. My mother called twice, but I was on the phone setting up my summer internship and had missed her calls. She reached me on the third call, and it was, of course, the dreaded phone call that no one wants to get. I called my brother to tell him, and then it became very clear to me that it would only be a matter of time before the process of grief would begin. We started calling family members to inform them of Auntie's passing. It was the routine course of action when a family member passes. You call people, you let them know what's going on, you make travel arrangements—but nothing made sense. It did not register. I just did what I was supposed to do in a cloud of functional robotics.

Wednesday, April 20: Numbness, Quiet, and Deafening Silence

It had not settled in yet. In talking with my grandmother, she said that the night Auntie died, she prayed and placed Auntie into God's hands. A few minutes after her prayer, Auntie took her last breath. That was it. She was gone. "I hated to see her go, but I didn't want her to suffer anymore," my grandmother shared. She remained calm; the hospice team had prepared her for what to do when this time came. She called the hospice number and said, "I think I need you guys." The hospice staff arrived and made the necessary arrangements.

Saturday, April 23, 2005: Funeral

Auntie's funeral was held in Shreveport at her home church of over thirty years. I made it through my scripture reading of 2 Corinthians

5:1–9. It was a beautiful service. I was doing well until suddenly, out of nowhere, what felt like the prick of a hot needle in the middle of the back of my head was grief's way of announcing its presence. Grief crept up from that point in the back of my head and radiated out like a tsunami, which quickly engulfed my face. It felt tingly, and it felt hot. I then felt the overwhelming burden of emotion rendering me inconsolable. As with many African American churches, when one is overcome by grief, there is a team of folks who will surround you, rub your back, fan you, give you a glass of water, and attempt to restore you to a sense of peace and well-being. Saying goodbye is never easy.

Reflections

Over the years, I have gained numerous insights, learned more about myself, and developed personally and professionally, as a member of clergy and a hospice chaplain, through myriad experiences both in my own life and through serving others. Whether we choose to realize it or not, each experience in life shapes us. The good, the bad, and everything in between will teach us a lesson if we remain open and allow ourselves to see the greater possibilities that await us.

My understanding of ministry has evolved over the years. I see things differently than I once did. I embrace new opportunities that allow me to serve others, to be a caring and compassionate presence, and to share the love of God while building relationships. I count it an honor to serve as a fellow sojourner on this journey of life with all people and helping to support those experiencing loss and grief. There is a dance, of sorts, that takes place. Some days we grieve; some days we journey with others in their grief. Some days it can be as simple as making space for another at the table or reflecting on your own journey with the courage to share your experiences that may inspire, strengthen, and remind others that they are not alone.

About the Authors

Pastor John J. Bergstresser: Pastor Jay attended the University of Central Florida, where he received a bachelor of arts degree in philosophy; was ordained to the Lutheran ministry in 1989; and went on to receive a master of divinity degree from the Lutheran Theological Southern Seminary in Columbia, South Carolina. He has served as a Lutheran (ELCA) pastor for the past twenty-six years, following his father into the ministry. He was  pastor at Grace Lutheran Church in Berwick, Pennsylvania (for six and a half years), and has been at Resurrection Lutheran Church in Cocoa Beach, Florida since 1996.

From 2001 to 2010, Pastor Jay served as a US Navy Reserve Chaplain, which formed much of his thinking as to the Jesus people need to know: the real, compassionate, radical Jesus of the Gospels. Among the many ministries carried out by his congregation, his favorite is street outreach to the homeless, which forms the basis for his book, *Strong Drink for the Perishing: Transformative Outreach to the Homeless.* Pastor Jay is married to Lisa Bergstresser, and they have two daughters, Anna and Renee.

Rev. C. Brandon Brewer, M.Div., CEOLS: Rev. Brewer is an associate team director and hospice chaplain at Seasons Hospice and Palliative Care in Columbia, Maryland. He is a graduate of the University of South Alabama in Mobile, Alabama (BS) and Columbia Theological Seminary in Decatur, Georgia (M.Div.). He is a Certified End-of-Life Specialist and is currently working on a doctor of ministry degree in pastoral care and counseling at Gardner-Webb University in Boiling Springs, North Carolina. He has over fifteen years of ministry experience having served as a chaplain, pastor, religious educator, youth minister, and

community college adjunct faculty member. For several years, he has worked to enhance the practice of chaplaincy and spiritual-care services in hospice by developing research strategies, tools, and presentations related to chaplain productivity, evidence-based spiritual care, culture, ethics, inclusion, utilization, leadership development, and spiritual considerations of African Americans at end of life. Because of his work, he has been invited to serve as a speaker and guest lecturer for local, regional, and national conferences. Brandon and his wife, Camille-Kay, reside in Annapolis, Maryland.

Rabbi Ari J. Goldstein: Ari Goldstein has been the rabbi of Temple Beth Shalom, a Reform synagogue in Arnold, Maryland, since 2004. He received his bachelor of arts from the University of Pittsburgh and his master of Hebrew letters degree and rabbinic ordination from the Hebrew Union College–Jewish Institute of Religion. He currently serves as the national chairperson of the synagogue division for Israel Bonds and leads many trips to Israel. He is married to Rabbi Hanna Yerushalmie and has four children—Sela, Nava, Sammy, and Judah.

The Rev. Torrence M. Harman: Rev. Harman is an Episcopal priest in the Diocese of Virginia. She re-cently retired at age seventy-two as rector of two historic rural churches in Lancaster County, Virginia, and currently serves as part-time priest-in-charge of two other historic rural churches a short distance away in Richmond County. Prior to ordination, she practiced law and mediation in Virginia for approximately twenty years. She is a spiritual director, leads groups and retreats, and serves as adjunct faculty teaching religion courses at Rappahannock Community College. She is married to J. W. ("Buff") Harman, a retired lawyer. They have five adult children between them and are grandparents to her nine grandchildren and his four. They live beside the beautiful Rappahannock River near where it flows into the Chesapeake Bay.

Michael J. Kurtz, PhD: Michael Kurtz serves as supply pastor at Magothy-Chelsea Community Lutheran Church in Pasadena, Maryland, where he has preached the Word of God for the past quarter century. Also, he is currently the associate director of the Digital Curation Innovation Center in the College of Information Studies at the University of Maryland. Prior to this, he worked for thirty-seven years as a professional archivist, manager, and senior executive at

the National Archives and Records Administration, retiring as assistant archivist in 2011.

He has published extensively in the fields of American history, contemporary spiritual life, and archival management. His works include *America and the Return of Nazi Contraband* (2006), *Rev. Robert B. Lantz: A Transformative Life* (2012), *John Gottlieb Morris: Man of God, Man of Science* (1997), *Call to Service: The Department of Patient Counseling, Virginia Commonwealth University, 1943–2013* (forthcoming); *The Journey of a Spiritual Traveler* (2016); and *Managing Archival and Manuscript Repositories* (2004). Michael Kurtz lives in Annapolis, Maryland, with his wife, Cherie Loustaunau, and their two cats, Samson and Delilah.

The Rev. John G. Lynch, PhD: John Lynch first served in the Roman Catholic church as a parish priest and seminary professor. He has now ministered as a pastor in the Lutheran tradition for over thirty years. While studying for his doctorate in theology in the 1960s, he learned many life lessons as a parish priest at St. Jean of Montmartre Christian community in the eighteenth district of Paris. He likes trips to the zoo with his wife, Kenne; walks with their toy poodle, Peaches; and novels by Ken Follett. Like  Luther, he also likes to polish up the Word of God.

Imam Mohamed Magid: Imam Magid is the Executive Imam of All Dulles Area Muslim Society (ADAMS) Center in Sterling, Virginia. He is the chairman of the International Interfaith Peace Corps (IIPC) and the former president of the Islamic Society of North America (ISNA). He also occupies the chair of the Fairfax County Faith Communities in Action and serves as the chairman of Muflehun, a think tank that focuses on confronting violent extremist thought through research-driven preventive programs within a religious paradigm. Imam Magid has a long history of commitment to public service through organizations such as the Peaceful Families Project.

Imam Magid has coauthored three books, *Before You Tie the Knot: A Guide for Couples; Reflections on the Qur'an;* and *Change from Within.* He has helped with training and work-shops for Imams and religious leaders, domestically and internationally, on the issue of violence against women. Imam Magid is leading an initiative to protect religious minorities in Muslim-majority countries through conferences where he conducts Imam  training on the Marrakesh Declaration. He has written for the *Washington Post* and the *Huffington Post* and has been profiled in *Time Magazine* and the *Wall Street Journal.* He is the recipient of the Washingtonian of the Year 2009 award and the Human Rights Award 2005 from Fairfax County.

Dr. Israel Zoberman: Rabbi Zoberman is the founding rabbi of Congregation Beth Chaverin and honorary senior rabbi scholar at Eastern Shore Episcopal Church, both in Virginia Beach, Virginia. He was born in Kazakhstan to Polish Holocaust survivors, emigrating to the American Zone in Germany, to Israel, and then to the United States.  Rabbi Zoberman has earned several academic degrees, with the distinction of being the only rabbi to earn a doctor of ministry degree in pastoral care and counseling from Chicago's McCormick Theological Seminary (1980), which is affiliated with the Presbyterian Church USA.

Rabbi Zoberman has been involved in numerous interfaith initiatives and has contributed to a variety of publications. He is a past national interfaith chair of the Jewish Council for Public Affairs (JCPA). Nobel Peace Laureate and Holocaust survivor Elie Wiesel has written about Rabbi Zoberman that, "As the son of Holocaust survivors, founder of his congregation in Virginia, and outspoken writer on Jewish and community issues, he has worked to keep memory of that tragic period in human history close in Jewish and American consciousness. Though respected for his spiritual leadership, he is equally sought for his erudition."

Rabbi Zoberman has been married to Jennifer Zeitlin since 1969. They are parents to Harel and Rachel (Ben) and proud grandparents to Danny and Andy.

Printed in the United States
By Bookmasters